Health Dimensions
of Economic Reform

World Health Organization
Geneva
1992

WHO Library Cataloguing in Publication Data

Health dimensions of economic reform

  1.Economic development   2.Health status   3.Public health
4.Social conditions

  ISBN 92 4 156146 7   (NLM Classification: WA 30)

This text was prepared for the International Forum on Health: a Conditionality for Economic Development, held in Accra, Ghana, on 4 to 6 December 1991, and was originally distributed as an unpublished document. In order not to delay its wider distribution, it is now being issued in published form without editorial revision.

Contributors to the document were: Dr S. Litsios, Dr R. Long, Dr K. Mott, Dr R. Thapa, Mrs D. Cooper Weil, the Steering Committee for the International Forum and the country teams. The work was carried out under the general direction of Dr A. El Bindari Hammad and Mrs C. Mulholland, with Mr G. Gunatilleke as principal editor.

The contributors and editors alone are responsible for the views expressed in this publication.

Designed by WHO Graphics
News clippings, collages and graphs by Marilyn Langfeld

Printed in Switzerland
92/9196 – Impressa – 4000

Contents

*Excerpts from the Constitution of
the World Health Organization*   *v*

Introduction   *vii*

Chapter 1
The outcomes of past development strategies   *1*

Chapter 2
The concept of vulnerability   *11*

Chapter 3
The role of functional literacy   *27*

Chapter 4
Linking economic well-being with health status   *37*

Chapters 5
Beyond the welfare-oriented approach   *51*

Chapter 6
Health as conditionality for development   *57*

Chapter 7
Conclusions   *63*

Excerpts from the Constitution of the World Health Organization

■ *The enjoyment of the highest attainable standard of health is one of the fundamental rights of every human being without distinction of race, religion, political belief, economic or social condition.*

■ *The health of all peoples is fundamental to the attainment of peace and security and is dependent upon the fullest co-operation of individuals and States.*

■ *Informed opinion and active co-operation on the part of the public are of the utmost importance in the improvement of the health of the people.*

■ *Governments have a responsibility for the health of their peoples which can be fulfilled only by the provision of adequate health and social measures.*

Source: World Health Organization, *Basic Documents,* 38th Edition, Geneva, WHO, 1990.

Introduction

Health is an essential objective of development. The capacity to develop is itself dependent on health. These two aspects of health and its links with development are now emerging with greater force and clarity. Health status cannot be traded off against economic gain. There is a better understanding of the crucial contribution of health to economic activity, to improvement of the human condition and, through these, to all the processes of development. The achievement of appropriate health objectives is therefore an important measure of the effectiveness of development strategies.

Awareness of the value of health for development was heightened during the economic recession of the 1980s, with the serious adverse consequences this had on the quality of life in developing countries. Policy-makers now pay closer attention to the impact that economic adjustment policies have on health and nutrition and are attempting to bring out more clearly than before the relationships between economic policies and health outcomes.

While there have been these special responses to the impact of adjustment policies, the same cannot be said of development policies in general. Despite the effects of development policies on health, the knowledge has not been systematically integrated into the process of policy-making. The impact that development policies have on health is seldom referred back to the policies themselves. Had this been done, policy-makers could have made adjustments that would have averted adverse health outcomes from the outset. Instead, there has been a continuing tendency to leave the emerging new health situations and problems within the domain of the health services. The main concern has been how the health services can deal with these situations and problems through expansion and improvement of their own capacity.

Development strategies therefore tend to attempt to reconcile the increasing burden of ill-health resulting from an accumulation of new health hazards with the escalating costs of health services and increasing sophistication of health technologies. Such a model of health care is proving impossible, even for the developed countries. It is biased in favour of the affluent and has already generated grave inequalities in access to health and health care. Its adoption by the developing countries would have disastrous consequences for the health of the vast majority of their populations. What is needed is a thorough reorientation of social and economic strategies, incorporating the health dimension at a more fundamental level in relation to selection of the options available for growth and development.

The problems of human health emerging as a result of the prevailing patterns of development are also assuming a global dimension. They are similar and closely linked to those that underlie the environmental crisis. The health issues, however, have an independent identity and must not be subsumed within the issues central to concern regarding the environment.

There has been some complacency with regard to ill-health following on industrialization, greater life expectancy, and the far-reaching changes in lifestyles and values now taking place. The complacency is mainly attributable to the expectation that advances in technology would be adequate to cope with the problems. Only recently have the global prospects for human health begun to disturb this complacency and attract the attention of the world community. The impact of environmental degradation on human health, the AIDS pandemic, the realization that modern transport and mobility promote the speedy transmission of disease, and some of the consequences of modern lifestyles detrimental to health have contributed to this awareness. The industrialized countries are now becoming aware of the magnitude of the health hazards that industrialization can generate and of how they accumulate and are often detected only after they have caused widespread serious impairment of human health. Many developing countries are confronted with a double health burden: not only must health authorities cope with the continued prevalence of malnutrition, diarrhoeal and respiratory diseases, and others such as AIDS and malaria, they must also face the emerging problems associated with industrialization, urbanization, and changing lifestyles, including occupational hazards, cardiovascular disease, cancer, drug abuse, and accidents. If this situation continues, it will give rise to a health crisis of unmanageable proportions.

The protection of health and the improvement of health status must therefore become essential conditions of socioeconomic policy. The term "conditionality" is used throughout this publication in a wide sense and applies both nationally and internationally. As it is currently used, it denotes the state of being subject to a set of economic conditions related to fiscal and exchange rate policies, the removal of subsidies, reduction in government spending, and other conditions that form part of the macroeconomic "discipline" imposed on borrowing countries by international lending agencies. The term has acquired certain negative connotations, since these policies when implemented have had severe adverse effects in the short term on the welfare of the vulnerable groups, especially in poor countries, even though the long-term effects are intended to benefit the economy and promote social well-being as a whole. Some population groups – the poor, women, and some communities – are especially vulnerable to the impact of these measures on their health status and quality of life.

If conditionality is considered in the specific context of economic adjustment, then "health conditionality" is the counterpart of economic conditionality. Action in response to the adverse social effects of adjustment policies has mostly been remedial in character and aimed at dealing with the effects, consisting of a few compensatory measures to bring some relief to the segments of the population that are adversely affected.

Conditionality has often been applied to lending for conventional projects and, in many cases, this has had social objectives. For example, utility projects often contain loan conditions aimed at extending water or other public services to the poor, often at subsidized rates. Environmental conditions attached to lending operations in a variety of sectors are often of benefit to the poor or disadvantaged, who tend to suffer most from environmental degradation.

Health conditionality is, however, wider in scope and more fundamental in character than remedial or project responses. It implies that the essential health objectives of protection and improvement of health status and quality of life should be defined at the very outset along with the macroeconomic objectives, and that the processes of adjustment should achieve both sets of objectives simultaneously.

For the developing countries, making health part of conditionality represents a more positive response to the basic issues of well-being that arise in the process of adjustment. However, health conditionality should not be restricted to the developing countries; it should be applied in all countries, since its aim is that the protection and promotion of health should be as much the primary objective of development as economic growth. Thus the objective of economic decision-making should from the beginning include the objective of protecting and promoting the quality of life.

A major issue that emerges at various points of the discussion in this publication is the role of the market. The approach that has been outlined relies essentially on the market for achieving its objectives, direct welfare-oriented state intervention being replaced by processes that increase the capacity of people for responsible decision-making. It therefore falls within the larger context of liberalization and restructuring of economic policy in which most countries are currently engaged. Four elements characterize this reorientation. First, the economic transformation of vulnerable groups involves increasing their self-reliance and enabling them to compete efficiently in the market. Second, households and communities should become increasingly responsible for the improvement of their health status and quality of life through access to health-related resources and as informed health consumers. Better flow of knowledge and information will promote this process. Third, public policy, through emphasis on health conditionality, should create the conditions for a health-promoting environment and provide incentives to that effect that align the market in relation to health objectives. Fourth, independent nongovernmental organizations, the media, and other groups safeguarding the interests of the public should play an important role in social decision-making.

The main themes in this publication are presented in the six chapters that follow. The argument put forward is that in setting general conditions for development any society needs to identify the areas of vulnerability in that society

and their acute manifestations in highly vulnerable groups. The book is arranged in the following order:

Chapter 1 is entitled "The outcomes of past development strategies" and briefly reviews the achievements of past strategies as reflected in the performance of developing countries during the 1980s. It provides the backdrop for an examination of some of the critical issues relating to health and development; the health situation of the vulnerable groups throughout the world providing the point of entry to such an examination as their health status is the best reflection of the development process.

Chapter 2 is entitled "The concept of vulnerability". This chapter defines the key elements in high vulnerability and indicates how the health status of vulnerable groups is an integral part of their economic well-being.

Chapter 3 is entitled "The role of functional literacy" and, with *Chapter 4* on "Linking economic well-being with health status", examines in greater detail some elements singled out as basic to strategies aimed at the transformation of vulnerable groups. In Chapter 3 the concept of functional literacy and its role are examined and in Chapter 4 the growth of productivity and economic enterprise in the vulnerable groups is discussed.

Chapter 5 entitled "Beyond the welfare-oriented approach" examines the larger issues involved in integrating health in development policy.

Chapter 6 on "Health as conditionality for development" looks at the implications of making health an essential condition of development at both micro and macro levels.

Chapter 7, the final chapter, summarizes the main conclusions.

Chapter 1
The outcomes of past development strategies

The performance of developing countries

Throughout the 1980s the poorest countries, with per capita incomes below US$ 500 (as defined in the World Development Report of the World Bank), had falling mortality rates and increasing average life span. Adult literacy rose. In aggregate terms the daily calorie supply increased marginally. In terms of food availability, health, and education, therefore, the outcome for this group of countries, taken together, recorded some improvement in well-being. But, as analysts have frequently pointed out, the figures used as aggregates for 42 countries with a population of 2950 million conceal sharp disparities. The population of China and India, for example, comprises two-thirds of this category; therefore, improvements in the health status of these two countries alone more than offset the poor performance of all the other countries put together. This can be seen in the aggregate data in Table 1, presented separately for India and China and the group of other low-income countries. When China is excluded, the average life expectancy drops from 62 to 57 years; when India is also excluded, it drops to 55.

In 1988 16 of the 42 countries in the group had an average life expectancy of below 50 years. This implies low child survival rates with infant mortality rates above 100 per 1000 live births. Twenty-six of the 33 countries for which data were available for 1985 had female illiteracy

Table 1: Development in low-income countries – selected indicators 1977-1989

	Population in mid-1989 (millions)	Life expectancy at birth (years)		Adult literacy (%)		Daily calorie supply per capita		Growth of GDP per capita 1980-1989
		1980	1989	1977	1985	1977	1988	
Low-income (a) countries excluding China & India	1002.0	48	55	34	49	2113	2182	0.7
China	1113.9	64	70	66	69	2441	2632	8.3
India	832.5	52	59	36	43	2021	2104	3.2
All low-income countries	2948.4	57	62	50	56	2238	2331	4.2
Mozambique (b)	14.9	47	49		38	1906	1595	-4.1
Bangladesh (b)	108.9	46	51		33		1927	0.9
Haiti (b)	6.3	53	55		38	2100	1902	-2.4

(a) Countries with per capita GNP of US$ 545 or below in 1988 and US$ 410 or below in 1980, as classified in the *World Development Report*, 1990 and 1982.
(b) The country with lowest per capita GNP (1988) has been selected from Africa, Asia, and Latin America.

Source: World Bank, *World Development Reports* 1982, 1990, and 1991.

rates above 50%. In 33 countries the crude birth rate was over 40 (per 1000 population). The marginal improvements therefore occurred in conditions in which the quality of life and the state of human development as reflected in health indicators remain extremely low.

Other developments in the 1980s heightened the risk to the health and well-being of the population in most poor countries. The economic base for protecting and improving health and well-being was seriously eroded as a result of adverse developments in the world economy and the consequent adjustments the poor countries had to make. Here again, there were wide variations in performance among the developing countries. Asian developing countries showed greater resilience in coping with the crisis and continued to maintain relatively satisfactory rates of growth, while many countries in Latin America and Africa suffered a significant decline in real per capita income. The per capita incomes of sub-Saharan Africa are estimated to have fallen by approximately 25% during the 1980s. Structural adjustment took a heavy toll of public expenditure. The resulting austerities and hardships contributed to social and political destabilization. The cuts imposed on health budgets further depleted and constrained services already quite inadequate to have the

desired impact on the existing poor health status. The allocation for public expenditure on health in 43 countries with a low human development index (as defined in the UNDP Human Development Report) has remained at 0.7% of the GNP during the past three decades. With the decline in GNP in absolute terms, the real per capita expenditure on the services has fallen. The levels of health expenditure would have been better able to protect and promote health if the development strategies that were adopted had not continuously added new hazards to the burden of ill-health and further distorted priorities in health care.

Survival with low quality of life

Improvements in health status and enhancement of the capacity for survival, even though marginal, have begun in the poorest countries to pose a new set of problems and challenges that have not yet been clearly identified or adequately understood (see box).

The initial outcome of lower mortality has been a rapid increase in population. While the average crude death rate for the poorest countries (excluding China and India) fell by 38% during the period 1965-1989, the crude birth rate dropped by only 13%. The decline in the total fertility rate was only marginal, from

Table 2: **Mortality and fertility in low-income countries (1965 and 1989)**

	Crude birth rate		Crude death rate		Total fertility rate	
	1965	1989	1965	1989	1965	1989
Low-income countries excluding China & India	46	40	21	13	6.3	5.5
China	38	22	10	7	6.4	2.5
India	45	31	20	11	6.2	4.1
All low-income countries	42	31	16	10	6.3	3.9

Source: World Bank, *World Development Report 1991*, Table 27.

Living longer but not better

The aging of populations is now a global phenomenon manifest in several parts of the world, incipient in all the rest.

The regional distribution of the population aged 60 and over reflects the growing tendency of the world's elderly to be concentrated in developing countries. The proportion of the world's aging population was evenly distributed between developing and developed countries from 1950 to 1975. By 2025, 72% of the elderly – about 858 million people – will be living in developing countries.

Lumping together the population aged 60 and above conceals two important factors: age and gender. In 1950 there were 13 million very old (defined as 80 years and above) in the world, constituting 7% of the total elderly population. In 1985 the number of very old had more than tripled to 45 million, 10% of the total elderly population, which only doubled during the same period. By 2025 the very old will number about 137 million, 11% of the total elderly. The increase in the 80-plus age group will be more rapid in developing countries. In both developed and developing countries, the 80-plus age group will grow twice as fast as the 60-plus age group.

There will also be a greater increase in the number of old women than of old men. Between 1985 and 2025 the projected increases for persons aged 70 and above are 32 million for males and 38 million for females in developed countries and 284 million for males and 317 million for females in the developing countries.

The conclusion is inescapable: the populations of developing countries will age, involve larger numbers, and age more rapidly than the populations of developed countries. Aging is usually regarded as a problem confined to developed countries. It is clear that in the future this will not be so. Aging is now a global problem, affecting developing countries as well as developed countries. The central policy implication, therefore, is that developing countries will have to plan for the increasingly rapid aging of their populations.

Source: United Nations Office at Vienna, Centre for Social Development & Humanitarian Affairs. *The World Aging Situation, 1991.*

6.4 to 5.6 during this period. With poverty and illiteracy persisting, women have had an increasing burden of child care and have had to cope with households of larger size.

More disturbing are the indications that the capacity for survival in the prevailing socioeconomic conditions is accompanied by adaptation to a poorer quality of life and increasing undernourishment, particularly among mothers, infants, and children. The technology and health care available appear to be able to sustain and prolong life in conditions of great deprivation. The proportion of babies with a low birth weight in a poor country with a relatively high life expectancy such as Sri Lanka – 28% of babies with a low birth weight and an average life expectancy of 71 years – is alarming evidence of this phenomenon (see Table 3, page 5).

Such projections call for a new look at development plans. Soon most of the world's elderly will live in developing countries, their lives often prolonged despite great deprivation.

The health dividend from economic growth

For the poorest countries, excluding China and India, average per capita incomes rose by approximately 40% during the period 1965-1989, while infant mortality declined by about 35%. It could be argued that, even within the relatively slow increase in economic well-being, improvement in health status as measured by infant mortality did not keep pace with economic growth. The health dividend of GNP growth (the share of the benefit accruing to health) in countries such as China and Sri Lanka has been much higher, that for India even poorer. The size of the health dividend reflects the differences in the ranking of priorities in the different development strategies and the sectoral mix of the investments undertaken.

Within these aggregates too, the rural-urban differentials remained high. National development strategies were inherently biased in favour of the small organized urban sectors in these countries. They did not adequately cover the poorer rural majority, and within this majority they tended to bypass the more vulnerable deprived groups. This is evident in some of the key indicators relating to the social infrastructure. Data reported at the end of the period show that, in the 44 developing countries that have the lowest indicators of human development according to the UNDP Human Development Report 1990, the share of the rural population having access to health services, safe water, and sanitation was 37%, 38%, and 6%, respectively. The comparable figures for the urban population in these countries were 81%, 74%, and 39%.

Within these rural-urban disparities the vulnerable population in the urban sector itself has continued to increase. The share of the urban population in the total population of the poorest countries, excluding China and India, rose from 14% to 25% during the period 1965-1989. This was not an orderly process in which the superior amenities available in the urban sector became available to the expanding population as a whole. Rapid urban growth has produced pockets of deprivation and subhuman conditions of living which are at times more severe than those to be found in the rural sector.

These development data help to identify the most vulnerable part of humanity. The population of the countries with the lowest socioeconomic indicators is estimated at approximately 1500 million. More than three decades of sustained development efforts have therefore failed to make a significant impact on the quality of life of a large part of the world's population. Neither the national development strategies that have been pursued by the majority of the poorest countries, nor the substantial flow of financial and technical assistance from the world community and international agencies, have yet succeeded in generating processes capable of rapidly transforming the quality of the deprived strata of their population.

Several international agencies have helped to promote strategies at the global and national level that attempt to reach these groups. WHO, with its goal of Health for All by the Year 2000, has drawn the attention of the world community to the fundamental issues of access to and equity in health and thereby promoted a basic reorientation of health strategies. Similarly, UNESCO with its goal of universal primary education, UNCTAD, UNDP, and other international agencies with their concern for the countries defined as the least developed, IFAD with its focus on the poorest populations in the agricultural sector, ILO with its programmes of employment promotion, FAO with its integrated rural development programmes, the World Bank with its emphasis on the alleviation of poverty, and UNICEF with its concern for the well-being of children, have all contributed to the development of policies and strategies that assign high priority to attacking the problems of the hard core of low income, illiteracy, and undernutrition, which have not yielded to past strategies.

Above all there is the growing realization that development incapable of reaching out to and transforming the disadvantaged and marginalized segments of society is flawed and incomplete from the outset.

Table 3: **Survival with low quality of life**
Selected indicators for Sri Lanka

Per capita GNP 1990, US Dollars	416
Life expectancy at birth in years, 1989	71
Female as percentage of male	106.1
Crude birth rate per 1000 population, 1989	21.3
Crude death rate per 1000 population, 1989	6.2
Total fertility rate per 1000 population, 1982-1987	2.8
Adult literacy, percent, Total 1988	87.0
Female 1988	83.0
Malnutrition	
Babies with low birth weight, percent, 1988	28.0
Wasting, percent, 1987	13.0
Stunting, percent, 1987	27.5
Anaemia among pregnant mothers, per cent, 1987	60.0
Causes of mortality	
Rate per 100 000 for the three disease groups with highest rates.	
Infants: Diseases of the respiratory system	264
Infectious & parasitic diseases including intestinal infectious diseases	219
Diseases of the nervous system	92
Total Population: Diseases of the circulatory system	37.9
Injury and poisoning	21.1
Infections and parasitic diseases	14.3

Sources: Ministry of Health, Sri Lanka, *Annual Health Bulletin*, 1990.
Department of Census & Statistics, Sri Lanka, *Demographic & Health Survey 1987*.
Central Bank of Sri Lanka, *Annual Report 1990*.

Missed opportunities for human development: the case of Brazil

Despite rapid economic growth and substantial meso interventions, Brazil's human development record has been unsatisfactory. The under-five mortality rate was still 85 per 1000 in 1988, almost twice Sri Lanka's and only slightly lower than Myanmar's, countries with per capita incomes amounting respectively to a fifth and a tenth of Brazil's. The life expectancy was 65 years in 1987, and the male and female literacy rates respectively in 1985 were 79% and 76%.

These national averages hide significant regional differences. In the poorer north-east, for example, infant mortality rates in 1986 were more than twice those in the rest of Brazil (116 compared with 52 per 1000), life expectancy at birth in 1978 was 49 years compared with 64, and prevalence of child malnutrition was twice the national average.

There are two important reasons for such poor demographic statistics in Brazil. One is the extreme inequality of income distribution. The other is inefficient targeting of public resources.

Well-structured meso policies can compensate for a poor distribution of income and improve human conditions. This has not happened in Brazil because public resources have not reached the poor or improved basic human development.

In health, preventive programmes such as immunization, prenatal care, and vector-borne disease control are estimated to be some five times more cost-effective than curative programmes in reducing mortality. But an estimated 78% of all public spending on health is allocated to largely curative, high-cost hospital care, mainly in urban areas and especially in the urban south. This is in sharp contrast to the 87% of public expenditure that Brazil allocated to preventive care in 1949, a share that fell steadily to 41% in 1961 and to a low of 15% in 1982 before rising to 22% in 1986. Similarly, more than a quarter of all public spending on education in 1983 went to higher education, only half to primary education.

Brazil thus demonstrates that substantial meso policy interventions, if poorly structured and badly targeted, cannot make up for an unequal distribution of income – even if the overall growth of income is more than adequate.

Source: United Nations Development Programme, *Human Development Report 1990*, pp 56-58.

Basic conditions of vulnerability

How can development strategies be designed to reach the disadvantaged segments of society and transform their conditions? The global data draw attention to a vulnerability structure which in turn indicates a critical path for reaching this objective.

Countries with a low ranking on the scale of human development invariably suffer from several combined forms of vulnerability. *They are deprived in relation to health, knowledge and education, purchasing power and income-earning capacity.* These forms of vulnerability exist within a general condition of powerlessness and lack of access to and control of resources. Almost all the poor countries are passing through a health transition stage in which mortality and fertility are high and life expectancy low.

The initial decline in mortality that occurs in this stage leads to a rapid increase in population. The average annual rate of population growth for these countries taken together increased from about 2% in the early 1950s to 2.6% in the period 1965-1980 and 2.8% in 1980-1988. But the avoidance of early mortality has not been accompanied by an increase in the capacity to promote and protect health. This includes the capacity to eliminate such risks as those encountered in repeated and teenage pregnancies, which contribute both to high maternal mortality and to population increase.

The fact that 60% of the population of the poor countries are still illiterate is one of the most important factors perpetuating this situation. The expanding population (population densities of 3900 per 1000 hectares are found in some instances) not only exerts pressure on the limited resources available but also, in the absence of technological progress, restricts the growth of productivity and income-earning capacity. The average per capita income of this group of countries was estimated at US$ 300 for 1987, and the prospects for a quick increase are bleak.

These forms of vulnerability cannot be considered in isolation from each other; they are inseparably linked and continuously reinforce each other in a vicious cycle. In the poorest developing countries, where agriculture is the largest economic sector, low human development exists primarily in the rural sector, in its most acute form in numerous widely dispersed small communities functioning with limited resources.

These forms of vulnerability are not confined to the developing countries. Similar situations are increasingly appearing in the industrialized world, such as teenage pregnancies and parenthood in the United States of America. In a recent study it was shown that teenage mothers are more likely to be unmarried, live in poverty, and remain so throughout their twenties (see box, page 9).

Yet Another Menace for the Third World

Alcohol is Making Underdevelopment Still Worse

To the familiar list of factors responsible for the low growth and social problems of the poor countries, another less well-known factor can often be added: alcohol....

In many households, the consequence of beer-drinking is that there is not enough money left for food and the children go to bed on an empty stomach. Moreover, alcohol has a much more drastic effect on the body of someone who is malnourished....

Generally speaking, in the countries where alcoholism is a problem, it is the men who drink and the women and children who suffer the consequences....

The vicious cycle of poor health, poor nutrition, low productivity and lack of the knowledge necessary in the context of change cannot be broken by action on any one of those elements independently of the others.

Low productivity derives from conditions in which poor health status has both short-term and long-term adverse effects on the manpower available. Low productivity and poor health status together derive from conditions in which households do not have the skills and information they need for developing the values and attitudes required to adapt successfully to the rapid changes that are taking place. These capacities must rest on an economic base that has the potential for increased productivity and purchasing power.

Vulnerable groups have, nevertheless, been able to evolve strategies for survival in conditions of extreme deprivation. This capacity indicates their potential for greater productivity, given adequate access to resources.

The development strategy that can transform vulnerable communities and lift them to a higher state of development will have to act simultaneously on all the conditions responsible for their vulnerability. The continuing impact that such a strategy has on the well-being of the household and the community will be the measure of its success. In it improvement of health status plays a vital role and becomes a critical indicator for the other inputs required for the process of transformation.

The focus on the most vulnerable groups

The need to identify community problems through the most vulnerable groups has universal application in any development situation and any society. This does not imply that development strategies must concern themselves exclusively or even primarily with raising the standards of such groups. Macroeconomic policies and strategies and national transformation through large-scale projects and investments no doubt provide the major thrust for structural change and economic growth. But structural problems that inhibit the process of development as a whole are reflected at the micro level because vulnerability is concentrated in the most disadvantaged segments of the population. Understanding the factors of vulnerability enables the necessary adjustments to be made to policies so as to prevent or mitigate vulnerability throughout the community.

Focusing on the most vulnerable groups is necessary as they have become a severe constraint on economic growth and development, the reason being that they tend to become marginalized in a strategy that relies mainly on the impetus imparted by large-scale national investment. Strategies that bypass these groups widen social and economic disparities and enlarge the hard core of vulnerability. This has

Teenage mothers in poverty

In the United States of America, one in three mothers aged 25-29 years who first gave birth as a teenager was poor in 1986, compared with one in six mothers of the same age who delayed childbearing until after the age of 20.

In 1988 both the number of births to teenagers and the birth rate among teenagers increased. The increase in the birth rate was for the second successive year. The rate increase was greatest for 15-17 year olds, for whom the rate rose from 31.8 births per 1000 to 33.8. These young mothers are even less likely than older teenagers to have finished high school or to be married, and their children confront greater health risks than those born to older teenagers.

Although death rates for babies born to teenagers are lower within the first 28 days after birth than for babies born to women in their twenties, the death rates within the first year of life are higher. Moreover, babies of mothers younger than 15 are at increased risk of low birth weight, which is associated with infant death and conditions such as cerebral palsy, autism, and learning disabilities.

Source: Children's Defense Fund. *The State of America's Children 1991*. Washington, DC, 1991, pp. 93-95.

Births to women younger than 20 in the USA, 1988

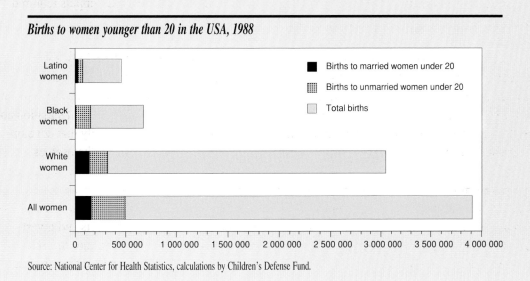

Source: National Center for Health Statistics, calculations by Children's Defense Fund.

to a large extent reduced the human resources available to the community and entailed great human suffering, which has manifested itself in the social discontent and political instability erupting in persistent civil disorder that characterize so many of these countries. For reasons affecting all the vital social, economic, and political goals of development, development strategies can at no stage afford to neglect the most vulnerable groups in society and the need for their transformation.

What then does vulnerability signify? How can the vulnerable groups best be identified? Why does their transformation as productive human resources become so vitally important for the success of development strategies? What role does health have to play in them?

Kenya 1991

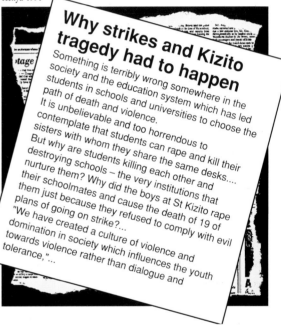

Why strikes and Kizito tragedy had to happen

Something is terribly wrong somewhere in the society and the education system which has led students in schools and universities to choose the path of death and violence.

It is unbelievable and too horrendous to contemplate that students can rape and kill their sisters with whom they share the same desks....

But why are students killing each other and destroying schools – the very institutions that nurture them? Why did the boys at St Kizito rape their schoolmates and cause the death of 19 of them just because they refused to comply with evil plans of going on strike?...

"We have created a culture of violence and domination in society which influences the youth towards violence rather than dialogue and tolerance," ...

Boston 1991

At Forum, Flynn Urges that Violence be seen as a "Public Health Issue"

..."Violence is a public health issue. It is one of the most difficult and complex problems facing the country today.... What is needed is a whole scenario for looking at the dynamics of the issue of violence." ...

The specialists issued recommendations that included a 25-cent tax on cigarettes to raise money for community health efforts and the formation of a coalition of institutions already established in the communities.

Chapter 2
The concept of vulnerability

The focus on health-related vulnerability

The concept of vulnerability has been widely used to denote a condition in which the physical and mental well-being required for a normal productive life is impaired and at constant risk. However, vulnerability in general usage includes any condition of exposure to hazards, risks, and stresses. It can, for example, be that of an economy highly dependent on a few primary commodity exports, of a firm in a rapidly changing market, or of the illiterate in an increasingly literate environment. This general definition of vulnerability has to be borne in mind in the discussion that follows.

The central concern here is with health-related vulnerability. Poor health status provides an initial entry to the condition of vulnerability. The health-related vulnerability of individuals and communities is reflected in patterns of morbidity, mortality, and reproduction, and is the product of various forms of social and economic deprivation acting simultaneously.

The concept of vulnerability itself is implicit in the concept of health risk, which has always been part of public health. The primary health care strategy was instrumental in extending the concept beyond narrow epidemiological considerations to basic conditions antecedent to disease and, outside the health sector, conditions that govern the capacity to resist ill-health and enhance immunity.

Experience in the application of primary health care strategies has helped to develop these concepts further and widen their operational scope. This has been possible through focusing on group vulnerability. Health risks manifested in epidemiological conditions and individual ill-health occur in groups of individuals or households exposed to a common set of conditions. These conditions are related to age, gender, locality, occupation, and other similar characteristics. The characteristics vary according to the health situation of the society concerned or the community within it.

The profiles of vulnerability

Vulnerability varies according to the level of development and the health transition stage of countries at any given time. While each society has its typical patterns for ill-health, within those general patterns, certain population groups and sections of society are exposed to the highest health hazards and have the lowest chances for survival and the poorest quality of life. These are the most vulnerable groups. Among these population groups are women in rural areas, unemployed youths, migrant workers, and teenage mothers.

The identification of groups of vulnerable people has enabled health researchers to place health status in total development and conceptualize health as a multisectoral product. National development strategies and the global system governing the economic and political relationships between nations have all contributed to the growth and perpetuation of vulnerability. Vulnerability manifested at the micro level has to be placed within these larger structures and

Women: a vulnerable group, especially in developing countries

Great progress was made in human and health development in the 1960s and 1970s, but the trend in the past decade has been towards growing disparities between the rich and the poor among and within countries. The number of people living in extremely adverse conditions has increased. For women in these circumstances the trend towards the "feminization of poverty" continues; one-third of all households are headed by single women and disproportionately fill the ranks of the poor.

 Despite some positive results from the United Nations Decade for Women, it has become clear that overall progress has been slow and patchy. The poor condition of women with regard to health and development generally persists or has deteriorated, though it is no longer seen as trivial or "merely" a question of prejudice, inequity and injustice, but as a major contributor to ineffective development.

The poor health status of women begins in childhood. Inequity between girls and boys is widespread, even at the level of sharing family resources such as food. As a result, most girls enter the reproductive age without the physical and social maturity needed for the tasks of bearing and raising children. More than 60% of pregnant women in Asia and Africa suffer from nutritional anaemia. Low pre-pregnancy weight and low weight gain during pregnancy are among the major factors causing low birth weight in developing countries. The incidence of low birth weight averages 15% in Africa and 20% in Asia, compared with 7% in developed countries. Low birth weight not only threatens the survival of children but also impedes their growth and development.

Existing and emerging factors such as maternal anaemia and malnutrition, drug and substance abuse, HIV infection and AIDS, sexually transmitted diseases and repeated unwanted pregnancies, combined with inadequate maternal and child health and family planning services, threaten both women's and children's chances of survival. The female child who survives infancy must still face the challenge posed by the long-term implications of the risk factors a woman faces as a result of her poverty, ill-health and lack of access to resources and services.

Sources: World Health Organization, *Women, Health and Development*, Progress Report by the Director-General for the 44th World Health Assembly, 4th April 1991, p2; *World Health Statistics Quarterly*, 38 (1985), 302-316; *World Health Statistics Quarterly*, 33 (1980), 197, 224.

systems, which extend beyond local boundaries to the national, regional, and global level. The strategies to deal with vulnerability have therefore to act at several levels – the local level, of the community and the households within it, the national level (in terms of sectoral and macroeconomic policies), and the global level (in terms of international policies and programmes relating to aid, technical assistance, and economic relations between countries).

At the same time, strategies that aim at reducing or eliminating vulnerability must not end up by substituting new forms of vulnerability for those already existing. For example, a poor farming community has to overcome the traditional health hazards of parasitic and communicable diseases, undernutrition, poor sanitation and unprotected water supply. It also has to deal with new health hazards entering its environment, such as pesticides, new agricultural

Child vulnerability in an industrialized state

The State of America's Children 1991, prepared by the Children's Defense Fund, shows dramatically that vulnerability is not confined to the low-income developing world. A probing analysis of growing child poverty and diminishing social services reveals that the numbers of vulnerable children and youths are reaching alarming levels.

Despite continuing improvements in the general economy, the child poverty rate in the United States of America rose in 1989 to 19.6%. A total of 12.6 million children now live below the poverty line, an increase of more than 2.5 million from a decade ago. The key underlying causes of child poverty are falling earnings and more families with female heads. Worker earnings have lagged behind the rising cost of living, the median wages of hourly workers falling by 29% between 1973 and 1989 among men younger than 25. In 1959, 23% of all poor families were headed by women. By 1989 that figure had soared to 52%.

The correlation between poverty and child health is borne out by statistics from the government-conducted 1988 national health interview survey:

- Children younger than 5 living in the poorest families are one-third less likely than children in more affluent families to be in excellent health.
- The gap is even greater for children older than 5 years. Poor 5-17-year-olds are about half as likely to be in excellent health as their more affluent counterparts.
- The poorest 5-17-year-olds lose 1.5 times more days of school because of acute or chronic health conditions.
- Poor children are twice as likely as affluent children to have physical or mental disabilities or other chronic health conditions that impair daily activity.

Perhaps the most dramatic situations are those facing homeless children – a growing phenomenon of the 1980s. Today families with children make up one-third of the homeless population. In some parts of the country they make up the majority. Nationwide, one in every five homeless persons is a child.

In one study of New York City's barrack-style shelters, 42% of parents interviewed said that they or their children, or both, had had diarrhoea for more than three days. Another study found that homeless children were twice as likely as poor children with homes to have elevated blood lead levels, a condition associated with developmental retardation. In Los Angeles 23% of homeless parents interviewed said that their children were often or always hungry.

Against this background vulnerability manifests itself in the form of:

- abused and neglected children: 2.4 million reported in 1989;
- children born drug-exposed: 375 000 drug-exposed infants born each year;
- children with emotional problems: 12% of all children younger than 18 suffered mental disorders in 1989;
- runaways: 450 700 children were described as runaways in 1988;
- homicide victims: homicide is now the second leading cause of death among all adolescents and young adults, and the leading cause among black youths.

Source: Children's Defense Fund. *The State of America's Children 1991*, Washington, DC, 1991.

technologies, pollution and other environmental ill-effects of large development projects, exposure to new lifestyles, drug addiction, and food substitutes of poor nutritional quality (e.g., tobacco, bottle-feeding as a replacement for breast-feeding, carbonated drinks as a substitute for local beverages of better nutritional quality).

Of equal, if not greater, importance is the emergence of AIDS in all countries. This pandemic has reached alarming proportions in the developing countries, where the health and social infrastructures are fragile and inadequately developed to handle the scope and magnitude of AIDS.

Health hazards: the price of industrialization

Malaysia experienced rapid and large-scale industrialization to such an extent that by 1977 42 rivers had become heavily polluted. Polluted water, combined with irregular rainfall, forced urban areas to ration the delivery of water. The shortage affected rural areas, forcing villagers to use water from rivers and irrigation canals. The result was a sizeable outbreak of cholera in 1978-79 (Rajeandran & Reich, 1981).

The poisonous industrial effluents that spilled into Malaysia's rivers killed many fish, leading to considerable economic losses in the 70 000-man fishing industry. Since fish accounts for 70% of the protein intake in Malaysia, depletion of supplies and rising prices led to nutritional problems for consumers as well as for fishermen. Heavy-metal contamination of shellfish and other fish was also reported at the same time.

Fish poisoned by industrial wastes continue to be of great concern to public health. Greater public awareness in the more industrialized countries and the development of more sensitive human health indicators are leading to earlier and in many ways more alarming evidence of the health consequences of water pollution.

One researcher scraped industrial pollutants off the bottom of a creek which contained fish suffering cancerous tumours; he placed this effluent on healthy fish, and produced identical cancers. The number of beluga whales in the Canadian St Lawrence River has decreased from over 5000 at the beginning of this century to fewer than 400 today. Most belugas suffer from cancers, birth defects, skin disorders and other crippling diseases. When their carcasses wash ashore they are so contaminated with toxic pollutants flowing from the Great Lakes, or from primary industrial plants operating near the river, that they are declared hazardous substances. Direct inference to human health is moot; however, cancer and birth defect rates increase as one moves west to east along the Great Lakes towards the St Lawrence River, and are highest among residents living on the river shores upon which the belugas beach themselves in death. Another study found that children of women who ate a diet high in Great Lakes fish during pregnancy suffer higher rates of growth retardation and learning disorders. The same effects are found in laboratory animals fed a diet high in Great Lakes fish (Labonte, 1991).

Sources: Labonte, R. Econology: integrating health and sustainable development. Part One: theory and background. *Health Promotion International.* 6: 49-65 (1991)

Rajeandran & Reich, M.R. Environmental health in Malaysia. *Bull. Atom. Sc.,* 37(4) 30-35 (1981)

Estimated/projected prevalence of AIDS in adults

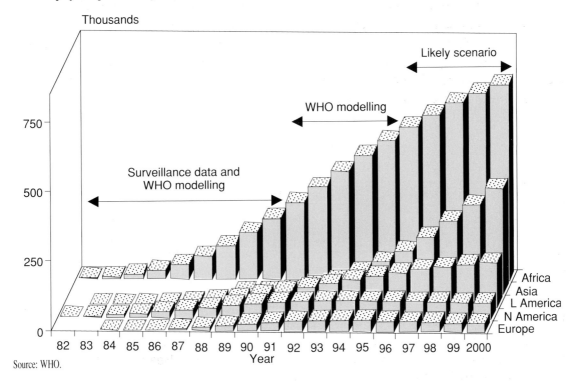

Source: WHO.

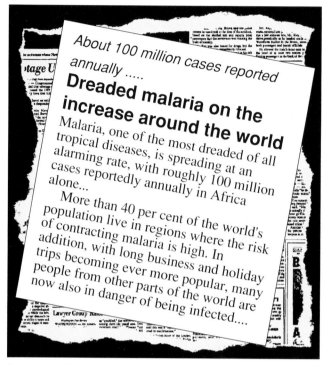

About 100 million cases reported annually .....

Dreaded malaria on the increase around the world

Malaria, one of the most dreaded of all tropical diseases, is spreading at an alarming rate, with roughly 100 million cases reportedly annually in Africa alone...

More than 40 per cent of the world's population live in regions where the risk of contracting malaria is high. In addition, with long business and holiday trips becoming ever more popular, many people from other parts of the world are now also in danger of being infected....

Development projects have resulted in resurgence of malaria in many countries.
Tourism and business travel are spreading the disease around the world.

Schistosomiasis – changing with the environment – highlights from 76 countries

Ghana
Since the construction of the Akosombo Dam (Volta Lake), intestinal schistosomiasis has been increasing in the Volta Delta.

Egypt
Since the construction of the Aswan Dam (Aswan Lake), intestinal schistosomiasis has dominated the Nile Delta and has spread towards Upper Egypt.

Somalia
Intestinal schistosomiasis is now in the north as a result of war and refugee migration.

China
Acute infections reappeared in Hubei and Hunan Provinces after 1988.

India
Urinary schistosomiasis was first reported near Hyderabad in 1989.

Philippines
Schistosomiasis has been reported in the deforested areas of Mindanao.

WHO 91769

Senegal
An epidemic of intestinal schistosomiasis (1987-1990) has been occurring in Richard Toll since the construction of the Diama Dam.

Urban schistosomiasis is now present in and around major cities in **Northeast Brazil** and **Africa**.

Botswana
Urinary schistosomiasis was reported in the Okavango Delta in 1989.

Mekong Basin
S. mekongi is now reported in new areas.

Source: WHO.

Estimated distribution of deaths from major diseases in 1985

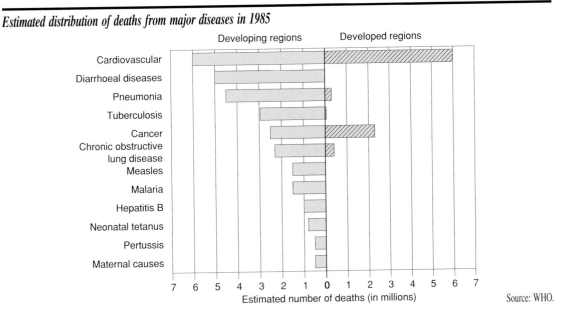

The above graph shows that industrialized countries have been able to reduce death from infectious diseases, while developing countries have to cope with mortality from infectious diseases and from noncommunicable diseases.

Methodologies for identifying the most vulnerable groups

Broad generalizations concerning the nature of vulnerability are helpful in defining this concept in concrete terms to render it more operational. A necessary initial step is to locate at the national level those areas or communities whose health and socioeconomic indicators are below the national average. The specific indicators for an in-depth analysis of these groups then have to be determined. From these, the causes of hard-core vulnerability have to be identified. The criteria and mix of indicators are different for communities at different health levels. Different types of households can be included to illustrate different kinds of extreme vulnerability. The choice has invariably to reflect high-risk conditions and therefore sensitivity to vulnerability.

The approach utilized in five African countries has several features of crucial importance in designing strategies of development (see box page 18).

The criteria that were selected have been particularly successful in defining a matrix of vulnerability. Identifying the most vulnerable group was to identify that part of the population in which all the elements of vulnerability converged: deprivation in health and physical well-being, in education and knowledge, and in income and economic well-being. These groups can be said to be in the condition of absolute vulnerability and provide an intersectoral measure that goes beyond the primarily economic measure of absolute poverty. While the measure of absolute poverty defined as a level of income insufficient to satisfy the minimum nutritional needs of an individual or household helps to identify the poorest groups in economic terms, it does not include the other forms of deprivation, which derive from the condition of extreme poverty and reinforce and perpetuate it.

Vulnerability is a composite indicator: it is an indicator of outcome as well as of processes.

Identifying a vulnerable group: women in Egypt, Ghana, Nigeria, Zambia and Zimbabwe

From the outset of the five country projects, it was agreed that women were to be the focus of attention since they represent one of the most vulnerable groups in these countries.

The search for the most vulnerable groups was undertaken in sequence from the national level to the local community. The first step was to identify the main regional disparities within the country, using the aggregate data. This led to the selection of one or more subnational units – province, district, or local government area – characterized by particularly low health and socioeconomic indicators.

In four countries the relatively disadvantaged subnational units were located in the rural areas. While the urban sector has aggregate indicators which, on average, are superior to those of the rural sector, pockets of vulnerability and deprivation exist that are not less severe than those of the most vulnerable groups in the rural sector. These urban pockets are exposed to urban and industrial pollution hazards in addition to other forms of social and economic deprivation. They manifest their vulnerability and their political volatility through social unrest. In one country, therefore, a typical urban situation of high vulnerability was also selected.

A multisectoral baseline survey undertaken in the project communities established a profile of the community services and infrastructure available, health status, health risk factors, educational levels, etc.

The indicators used to identify the most vulnerable women within the communities were the following:

1) Women in the reproductive age group;

2) Women who were illiterate regardless of the number of years of schooling;

3) Women who had lost a child to a preventable disease. This criterion showed the incapacity of women to prevent child deaths and provided an indicator of the utilization and accessibility of health services;

4) Women whose income level was considered to be below a community-determined poverty line. For this last indicator the community was necessarily involved in identifying those whom it considered to be the most vulnerable, since communities have their own way of determining those who are the worst off.

Identifying the most vulnerable women was only possible after intensive discussion with the community, in which the criteria and guidelines for identifying vulnerable households were worked out and the method of application and selection agreed upon between the community and the persons who were responsible for the project.

Finally, for management and monitoring at the community level, the precise location of the women identified as vulnerable was recorded on a map.

Source: Unpublished progress reports from 5 country projects.

In this sense the concept of vulnerability and the identification of vulnerable groups through its application define the actions that are vital for the transformation of the condition of the groups. This is shown in the form of a simple matrix illustrating the context utilized in the five countries (see page 20). The diagonal depicts the main elements of vulnerability; the rows indicate the combination of each element with the others and the columns the flow to each main element.

Measurement of the elements of vulnerability in a specific group is carried out in an ordered sequence. It is necessary to begin with the national average and identify the segment of the population below that average. The most vulnerable group is likely to be in the lower half of that segment or in the last two or three deciles of the total population ranked according to the indicators.

On this basis all countries will have groups that are relatively vulnerable. Their circumstances will provide the best insight into the problems of human development in their society and the corrective strategies that are needed. The sequence from the national level down through the different levels of society to the most vulnerable groups will enable the origins of vulnerability to be identified in the micro-economy and social structure of the local community, from which they can be traced back to the national economy and the international environment where adjustments must be made.

The following examples from each of the five countries participating in the project "Promoting Health Through Women's Functional Literacy and Intersectoral Action" highlight the specific aspects of vulnerability in the project communities.

Nigeria

In Nigeria the infant mortality rate is estimated at 110 per 1000 live births, the maternal mortality rate at 16 per 1000. About 10% of children are expected to die before their fifth birthday and one out of every four children born to a woman will die before she reaches the end of her reproductive life.

In Nigeria the local government areas of Agagbe in Benue State and Kataerigi in Niger State are among those classified as depressed and disadvantaged. In Agagbe 98% of the population surveyed obtained water from streams or springs and often had to walk long distances to them in the dry season. In Kataerigi 37% of the population surveyed were more than 10 km from a health facility.

Female illiteracy in the local government areas of Agagbe and Kataerigi stands at around 80%, and behaviour and practice are not conducive to good health. The majority of the people do not understand the relationship between malaria and mosquitos or the health risk to an infant of cutting an umbilical cord with a contaminated razor.

Zimbabwe

In Zimbabwe the project is located in Chivi district, Masvingo Province. Chivi district is a drought-prone area where the mean annual rainfall is between 300 and 700 mm.

Economic activity in the 26 administrative wards that make up Chivi district consists mainly of subsistence farming.

Poverty is the most widespread pervasive risk factor in the vulnerability of people living in Chivi. About 60% of the project population have individual annual incomes of below

Matrix of vulnerability

	Health	Education	Income-earning capacity	Power & control over resources	Living environment & physical infrastructure
Health	High infant/child/maternal mortality. High chronic/acute malnutrition. High fertility, birth spacing inadequate. High incidence of parasitical communicable diseases. Low average life span.	Low school participation/poor attendance. Link between home & school, through health, poor or absent. Health contribution to school curriculum poor.	Low productivity, poor care and maintenance of human capital. Loss of working time. Income effects of high fertility and increasing household size.	Gender discrimination in health care, neglect of potential for collective action and association in health affairs, pre-school children, maternal health, nutrition.	Neglect of link between environment and health. neglect of quality of habitat.
Education	Inadequate knowledge on – family planning, child/ maternal care, nutrition, health illiteracy, poor access to health messages.	Low school participation. No adult or functional education. High adult illiteracy. Access to non-formal education poor.	Limited or no access to new knowledge/technology for economic activity, managerial knowhow, entrepreneurial skills.	Lack of knowledge for coping with increasingly literate environment, lack of access to knowledge needed for control & management of resources, collective action, building institutions.	Inadequate knowledge of personal and household hygiene, and health implications of housing, water, sanitation.
Income-earning capacity	Inadequate income/output to satisfy minimum food needs/health care needs/ maintain & improve human capital.	Low priority for education. Limited access to educational resources. Low school participation.	Poor economic base and lack of income earning assets/resources.	Lack of access to and control over economic resources.	Lack of savings and capital formation for improvement of community and household infrastructure.
Power & control over resources	No or limited decision making power within household & community – family planning, food distribution, collective action for health.	Gender discrimination in access to education. Low priority for education. Poor access to educational facilities.	No capacity for aggregating common economic interests & mobilizing for collective action on economic activity, credit, marketing.	Inadequate community leadership, lack of institutions for aggregating common interests and for collective decision making.	Low level of collective action and community participation.
Living environment & physical infrastructure	Parasitic, water-borne disease, diarrhoeal, acute respiratory infections.	Link between school and habitat not used. Poor contribution to school curriculum.	House as potential for workplace not utilized. Employment in housing and infrastructure not used.	Failure to utilize scope for collective action and community participation for improvement of habitat.	Poor housing, poor sanitation, lack of protected water supply.

Source: G. Gunatileke: An analytical framework drawn from profiles of vulnerability in five developing countries.

Z$ 400 and the possibilities of viable economic activities in the drought-stricken and impoverished area are few.

In the six (out of 26) wards that were chosen for the project, the level of women's education is very low, 20% of women never having been to school at all, and 21% having at most four years of formal schooling. In the 15-45-year age group 25% of the women were found to be completely illiterate.

The functional nature of the women's illiteracy is illustrated by the fact that, while 99% of women knew about the home management of diarrhoea using salt and sugar solution, only 30% knew the correct proportions of salt, sugar and water.

Factors putting infants, children, and mothers particularly at risk in Chivi district include the lack of communications and transport and the distances to be travelled for such essentials as water and firewood. Women walk up to 10 km to the nearest water source, and as a result of deforestation have to go further and further afield for firewood.

Ghana

The two districts, Dangme East and Ho, which were selected for the project in Ghana, are truly representative of disadvantaged areas because of their physical environment and their social, economic and health problems.

The following indicators of the vulnerable condition of women came to light during the baseline survey:

- Illiteracy rates attained 80%.
- There was poor health knowledge about the causes, prevention and treatment of common ailments such as diarrhoea, dracunculiasis, convulsions and the six childhood killer

diseases. Risk behaviour included treatment of newly cut umbilical cords with sand and deliveries by untrained traditional birth attendants. The result was a high incidence of maternal and infant mortality and morbidity.
- Improper disposal of refuse, indiscriminate defecation, and unpenned livestock resulted in poor environmental sanitation.
- The economic status of the area was very low. Most vulnerable women had an income below the poverty level (less than 30 000 cedis per annum, or approximately US$ 176) and no employable skills.

Zambia

In Zambia the project is located in Mumbwa district, which lies about 157 km west of Lusaka in Central Province. Three wards (Nalusanga, Kapyanga, Mpusu) were selected as representing communities with different characteristics in relation to means of subsistence, environment, and access to health services.

In all three wards more than half the women were found to be illiterate, Mpusu having the highest illiteracy rate, 73% of the women. This is a result of the lack of schools in the area.

The overall crude death rate in the project area was estimated at 13.6 per 1000 population, Mpusu having the highest crude rate, 28.7%. Among the main causes of death cited were malaria, and diarrhoea with vomiting. Only 43% of the population surveyed had access to safe water. Over half of the women did not know what the cause of diarrhoea was.

In about half of the households in the project area, food production was inadequate to meet the demand. Children were rarely fed more than once or twice a day owing to lack of food and lack of resources to buy any.

Egypt

The table below dramatically portrays the vulnerability of the project site in Egypt and its inhabitants when compared with national averages.

Table 4A: The vulnerability of the chosen area as representative of urban depressed areas on the national scale

Criteria		Project area	Country level[1]
Persons/room average		3.9	1.4
One-room household		100.0%	12.6%
Garbage disposal, periodicity			
	once/week	0.0%	38.5%
Toilet facilities per household		0.0%	57.4%
Insect vectors prevalence		88.1%	4.7%
Bathing frequency			
	once a week	51.4%	21.0%
	twice a week	32.1%	39.7%
Measles vaccination		65.4%	74.9 %
Illiteracy:	males	63.4%	35.2%
	females	90.2%	81.7%
Unemployment:	males	29.5%	
	females	19.7%	

[1] Urban

Table 4B: Profile and character of vulnerable groups

Characteristics		Project area	Country level
Children below 5 years		12.7%	11.0%
Deliveries:	home	65.5%	
	dayas	52.8%	
Unemployment:	males	29.5%	
	females	19.7%	
Females aged 5-14		14.4%	12.8%
Females aged 15-45		24.4%	24.9%
Prenatal care: none		67.0%	
Tetanus immunization: complete		33.8%	
Weaning: sudden		76.2%	
Scabies prevalence		25.1%	

Through this process the most acute symptoms of ill-health or the propensity for poor development in the total system come to light. The most vulnerable group is the microcosm in which the propensity for affliction in the system appears as a whole in its most acute form. The existence of these groups, their size, and the nature of their vulnerability are both an indicator of the society concerned and a measure of the incapacity of past and ongoing processes of development to reach out to and transform these deprived communities. Health status is the best point of entry into this matrix of vulnerability because of its links to all other forms of vulnerability. It is also the best indicator of progress in moving out of the condition of vulnerability. The process described is indispensable for adopting effective strategies of human development.

Four clusters of health indicators

A wide range of indicators can be used for defining health status in all its varied characteristics. First is the cluster directly related to disease – the types of disease, their incidence, and the rates of morbidity. These help to define the prevailing pattern of morbidity and identify the diseases that cause the major health problems. They are also useful for reflecting the quality of the health care available, the infrastructure of the curative, preventive, and rehabilitation services, and the quality of the physical environment, including water, housing, and sanitation.

The second set of indicators relates to the conditions immediately antecedent to disease, frequently referred to as risk factors. Examples include malnutrition (undernutrition in its various forms, obesity, low birth weight), reproductive health such as birth spacing and fertility rates, levels of immunization, smoking, and alcohol and drug abuse.

The third set is the mortality indicators. Rates of mortality broken down by age, sex, and other relevant characteristics are among the most revealing indicators of extreme vulnerability. All the major forms of deprivation contribute to the high mortality rates.

The fourth set is the process indicators. The indicators of health status must include those that relate to the processes that contribute to health status outcomes and human development.

They include not only the quality of the health services, access to them, and the extent to which they are utilized, but also the inputs of education, the immediate health environment of housing, water, and sanitation, the work environment, and the income and purchasing power.

The aim is to contribute to the maintenance and enhancement of human resources, through a higher rate of survival, an increased life span, improved working capacity, higher work output, and greater productivity.

Estimated trends in mortality for major causes of death, 1970-1985

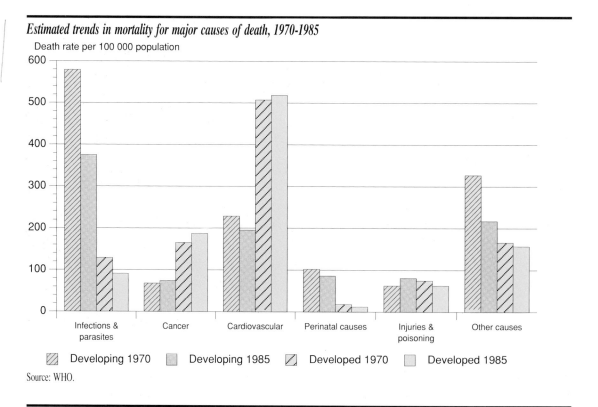

Death rate per 100 000 population

Developing 1970　　Developing 1985　　Developed 1970　　Developed 1985

Source: WHO.

Maternal mortality rate per 100 000 live births: a comparison of age groups

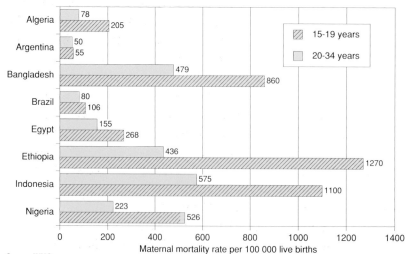

Source: WHO.

Childbearing at any age involves some risk. Maternal mortality rates in the developing countries average about 450 per 100 000 live births as compared with 30 per 100 000 in developed countries. The risk increases for young women. In Jamaica and Nigeria it has been found that pregnant women younger than 15 years are 4-8 times more likely to die during pregnancy and childbirth than pregnant women aged 15-19. In the USA in 1977 the maternal death rate among mothers under the age of 15 was 2.5 times higher than the rate among mothers aged 20-24.

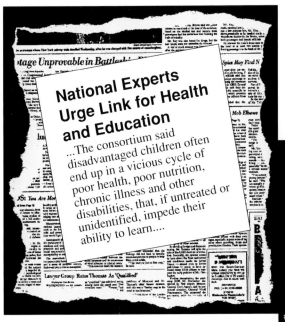

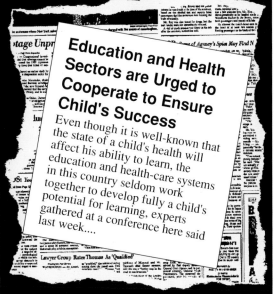

A better link between education and health can help break the vicious cycle of poor health and nutrition, chronic illness, and learning and other disabilities in which disadvantaged children find themselves.

Beyond the primary health care strategy

The indicators discussed contain the main elements of the primary health care strategy. That strategy emphasized the importance of water and sanitation, information, agricultural extension, and other services designed to protect and improve health status. It also stressed the need for intersectoral action and the importance of focusing on vulnerable groups. However, the constraints imposed by national administrative systems and decision-making processes prevented the strategy from extending beyond the health services and their field of operation in so far as to make the intersectoral component fully effective. Moreover, in emphasizing the various elements needed for primary health care as a whole, the strategy did not focus attention

adequately on the reasons why certain population groups did not have access to its elements.

In the approach developed in the five country projects, the strategy has been taken further. The structural nature of vulnerability has been made more explicit. The continuing interaction between health status and the socioeconomic situation assumes greater importance. The causes depriving vulnerable groups of the capacities and resources needed for their transformation are explored more fully. Analysis of the condition of vulnerability opens the path to the other larger issues of health conditionality considered later in this publication. Unless these larger issues are addressed, the intersectoral approach itself is likely to remain ineffectual.

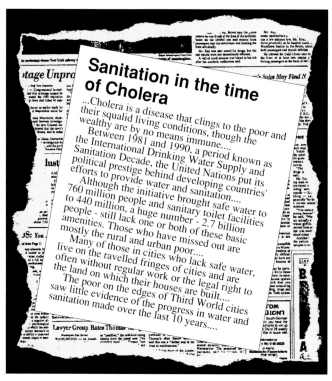

Sanitation in the time of Cholera

...Cholera is a disease that clings to the poor and their squalid living conditions, though the wealthy are by no means immune....

Between 1981 and 1990, a period known as the International Drinking Water Supply and Sanitation Decade, the United Nations put its political prestige behind developing countries' efforts to provide water and sanitation....

Although the initiative brought safe water to 760 million people and sanitary toilet facilities to 440 million, a huge number - 2.7 billion people - still lack one or both of these basic amenities. Those who have missed out are mostly the rural and urban poor....

Many of those in cities who lack safe water, live on the ravelled fringes of cities and are often without regular work or the legal right to the land on which their houses are built....

The poor on the edges of Third World cities saw little evidence of the progress in water and sanitation made over the last 10 years....

Cholera is a disease of poverty. It may indicate the quality of the housing, water, and sanitation available.

Countries, or areas within countries, reporting cholera in 1991, as at 30 August 1991

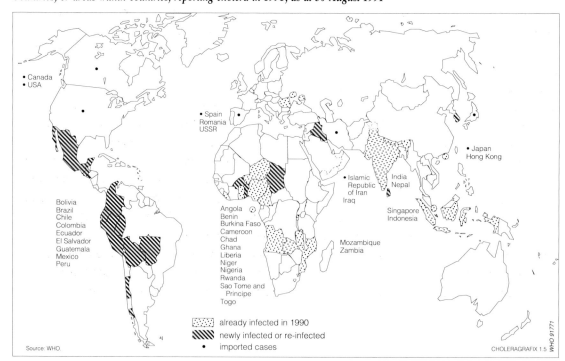

Canada
USA

Spain
Romania
USSR

Japan
Hong Kong

Bolivia
Brazil
Chile
Colombia
Ecuador
El Salvador
Guatemala
Mexico
Peru

Angola
Benin
Burkina Faso
Cameroon
Chad
Ghana
Liberia
Niger
Nigeria
Rwanda
Sao Tome and
Principe
Togo

Islamic
Republic
of Iran
Iraq

India
Nepal

Singapore
Indonesia

Mozambique
Zambia

- already infected in 1990
- newly infected or re-infected
- imported cases

Source: WHO.

CHOLERAGRAFIX 1.5

WHO 91771

Chapter 3
The role of functional literacy

The scope of functional literacy

Illiteracy is a major barrier for those seeking improvement in health status and quality of life. For many vulnerable people illiteracy is not only a barrier to communication, understanding, and knowledge, it is also a condition that prevents them from seeing the world beyond their immediate surroundings. Without the ability to read, access to a basic knowledge of health and strategies for improvement are beyond their reach.

Functional literacy must therefore be seen as an integral part of any national strategy for improving the condition of the most vulnerable groups. But functional literacy is different from primary education. The goals of basic education are common to both, but functional literacy also includes the life skills and specific knowledge needed to survive and function in any society. It is an essential tool for the future of the individual, family, community, and nation. Each adult who becomes literate is more likely to emphasize the need for the children to attend school and learn to read. Literacy expands horizons.

Basic illiteracy, the inability to read, write, and count, receives the attention of most functional literacy programmes. Illiteracy denies access to the vast body of information and knowledge that is being continuously conveyed in written form and which is essential to households and individuals in dealing with the increasingly literate and numerate world around them. Consequently the basically illiterate lack the skills needed for elementary contact with the external world around them, if only to read a public notice, a health poster, a road sign, or a letter, or to carry out a simple monetary transaction. Illiteracy means lack of the basic tools needed for the continued learning and self-education that are both possible and necessary in the rapidly expanding world of knowledge and information. It also limits the ability to analyse and deal with other forms of non-written communication.

The non-literate are therefore condemned to remain in a world of oral communication. The main task of functional literacy is to provide a bridge from that traditional oral world to the modern world of literate and numerate knowledge and skills.

In this context, functional literacy is fundamentally different from formal education, in which the basic skills are imparted in the early years of life and the teaching and learning methods and course content are related to the child's world and experience. In functional literacy, the basic skills are acquired by an adult for the purpose of application to the living and working environment. From the start, therefore, a group has to recognize the close links between learning and the situations with which it has to deal in daily life.

Learning to live better: the five country cases

In the five country projects there were three linked objectives for introducing functional literacy. First, the programmes aimed at equipping women with the knowledge and skills needed to protect and improve the health status of the household. The education included information relating to nutrition and physical fitness, preventive health, response to illness, and protection and improvement of the immediate physical environment.

Second, programmes aimed at providing the required information and managerial skills to use all available resources and technology efficiently so as to increase productivity and raise incomes and purchasing power. Third, functional literacy was seen as a process of empowerment. It enhanced the knowledge and understanding needed to identify the sources of vulnerability and consider options for action. It increased the capacity of vulnerable groups to exercise choice and to take decisions on matters affecting their well-being, and it created an appreciation of the value of good health as an essential aspect of well-being.

The programmes were multisectoral and multipurpose. By relating the teaching of basic skills to critical factors of vulnerability, functional literacy became an avenue for the provision of the essential knowledge and life skills required for the women to lift themselves out of their vulnerable condition.

Source: Unpublished progress reports from 5 country projects.

Functional literacy and behavioural change

Functional literacy can be a genuine development education, with far-reaching impact on the transformation of the human condition. For example, in the existing knowledge structures of the groups, knowledge relating to health is part of a world view and set of beliefs that include the origins of ill-health and modes of cure.

A basic knowledge of the cause of disease or of desired changes in behaviour patterns calls for major adjustments in knowledge and beliefs. These have to be approached with great care and sensitivity. Cultural resistance can lead to distortion and rejection of the new knowledge and the attitudes and practices that go with it. Exposure to new knowledge can cause the disintegration of old structures and their replacement by lifestyles, values, and attitudes that impair health and bring new health risks. Food substitutes, new technologies such as the use of pesticides and other agrochemicals in the rural areas, the importance of personal behaviour in the spread of diseases such as AIDS, and environmental pollution and degradation are all examples of what households and communities need to be informed about so that they can benefit from all the practical safeguards available.

Illiteracy can be deadly

The wiping out of a Zimbabwe family - six died after eating contaminated maizemeal, following the spraying of their huts to get rid of insects - could have been avoided if the villagers had even basic awareness of the deadly danger of pesticides....

This Zimbabwe family lacked the information it needed to cope with chemicals new to its daily life.

These high school graduates may know how to read, write and count but they lack the knowledge and skills required to cope with work and life

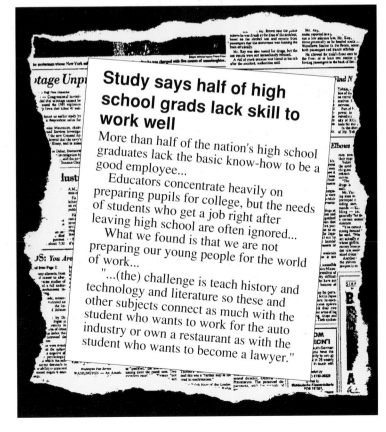

Study says half of high school grads lack skill to work well

More than half of the nation's high school graduates lack the basic know-how to be a good employee...

Educators concentrate heavily on preparing pupils for college, but the needs of students who get a job right after leaving high school are often ignored...

What we found is that we are not preparing our young people for the world of work...

"...(the) challenge is teach history and technology and literature so these and other subjects connect as much with the student who wants to work for the auto industry or own a restaurant as with the student who wants to become a lawyer."

While some of these measures require action at the national and sectoral level, functional literacy must enhance knowledge and awareness of hazards and strengthen the capacity to respond to them appropriately at the level of the household and the community.

The wider application of functional literacy

Functional literacy programmes have wider implications for the management of development and social change. Their basic elements in the situations described are applicable to other situations of high vulnerability with different combinations of health status, income, and education. They need not be confined to vulnerable groups absolutely illiterate in the sense that they are unable to read, write, and count; they also apply to groups that have had

formal education but have not been equipped with the basic capacities and life skills needed to cope with their specific forms of vulnerability. Educational programmes to equip them with the required basic capacities and skills have to be designed as programmes of functional literacy, appropriate to their condition of vulnerability.

In industrialized societies the link between poor health status and socioeconomic conditions needs to be established and incorporated appropriately in educational programmes. This is particularly important in relation to vulnerable youth groups throughout the world in which drug addiction, health-impairing lifestyles, problems of adolescence, and unemployment coexist in different combinations.

*Table 5: **Dimensions of health behaviours – factor analyses of selected health behaviours among 15-year-old pupils in 9 countries** [1]*

	Norway (n=1291)		Finland (n=1098)		Sweden (n=1077)		Scotland (n=1597)		Austria (n=1134)		Wales (n=2069)		Hungary (n=1267)		Belgium (n=1118)		Israel (n=991)	
	F1	F2	F1	F2	F1	F2	F1	F2	F1	F2	F1	F2	F1	F2	F1	F2	F1	F2
Alcohol monthly	0.76		0.77		0.67		0.53		0.70		0.74		0.73		0.59		0.70	
Smokes weekly	0.73		0.76		0.66		0.64		0.63		0.61		0.68		0.64		0.47	
Coffee weekly	0.57		0.43		0.60		0.53		0.59		0.50		0.51		0.42		0.60	
Unhealthy food (sumscore)	0.58		0.51		0.58		0.52		0.46		0.25(-48)		0.42(52)		0.55		0.38	
Healthy food (sumscore)		0.69		0.74		0.74		0.69		0.73		0.70		0.68		0.70		0.67
Oral hygiene (sumscore)		0.66		0.54		0.63		0.57		0.64		0.45		0.51		0.53		0.73
Vitamins daily		0.60		0.55		0.53		0.45		0.25		0.53		0.50		0.48		0.34
Physical activity (2+ hours/week)		0.48		0.48		0.36		0.44		0.40		0.26		0.40 (0.24)		0.27		—
Proportion of variance	41.4%		38.4%		37.2%		36.2%		34.6%		33.8%		33.1%		32.0%		30.3%	

[1] Principal components analysis with varimax rotated factor matrix

Source: World Health Organization, *World Health Statistics Quarterly* Vol. 44 No. 2, 1991, p. 58

Prevalence of smoking among young men and young women

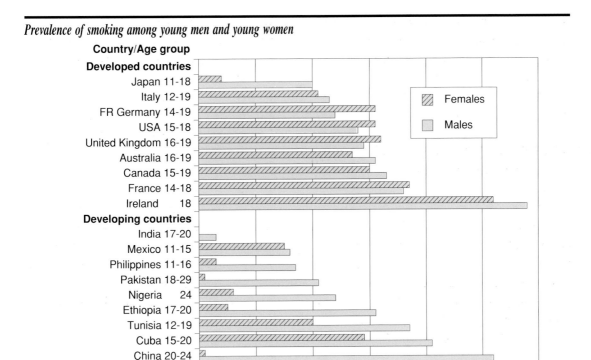

Country/Age group

Developed countries
- Japan 11-18
- Italy 12-19
- FR Germany 14-19
- USA 15-18
- United Kingdom 16-19
- Australia 16-19
- Canada 15-19
- France 14-18
- Ireland   18

Developing countries
- India 17-20
- Mexico 11-15
- Philippines 11-16
- Pakistan 18-29
- Nigeria   24
- Ethiopia 17-20
- Tunisia 12-19
- Cuba 15-20
- China 20-24

Females
Males

Around 1985
Various sources

% currently smoking

Source: WHO.

Teenage behaviour threatens health

Of great concern are the one-quarter of American adolescents who engage in high-risk behaviour that endangers their own health and well-being and those of others as well. These 7 million young people have multiple problems that can severely limit their future: most have fallen far behind in school, and some have already dropped out; some have been arrested or have committed serious offences; and typically they are frequent and heavy users of drugs and alcohol.

Adolescents engage in unprotected sexual activity, and some have experienced pregnancies or contracted sexually transmitted diseases. Sexually active adolescents have the highest reported rates of sexually transmitted diseases (STDs) of any age group. An estimated one in seven teenagers currently has an STD. Overall, approximately 2.5 million are infected with an STD each year. In 1989 there were 1123 reported cases of gonorrhoea for every 100 000 adolescents aged 15 to 19. Experts report that the average gonorrhoea rate in black males in this age group is about 15 times that of their white counterparts, and that the rate for black females of that age is 10 times the white rate.

Special efforts must be made to reach these young people early and provide them with both the means and motivation to avoid risky, dangerous and destructive activities that threaten their prospects for a satisfying adult life, their families and their communities.

Sources: National Commission on Children. *Beyond Rhetoric – A New American Agenda for Children and Families*, Washington DC, 1991, p. 220.

Children's Defense Fund. *The State of America's Children 1991*, Washington DC, 1991, p. 94.

In this way functional literacy, with its problem-solving participatory methodology, inculcates the capacity for continued learning and self-reliance in education that are essential for the constant adjustments and responses to changes and fresh hazards that must be made in adult life. By itself the process brings about a qualitative change, imparting a sense of confidence and self-reliance.

Ability to cope through access to relevant information

Vulnerable groups in countries have their own specific forms of functional illiteracy, which are an intrinsic part of their condition of vulnerability. For example, rapid technological change and new products and services create new forms of ignorance and functional illiteracy, requiring a continuous flow of new information and basic knowledge.

In this context, a regular flow of information to the public in general and vulnerable groups in particular assumes critical importance. Consumer education, with its impact on individual preferences and demand and its correction of distortions of the market that impair health, is illustrated by the action of many industrialized countries on, for example, the problems of unhealthy lifestyles and pollution. The success of the movement for physical fitness and a healthy diet is another example of the way in which people with the relevant information adopt more responsible behaviour and practices (see collage pages 34 and 35).

Historically, literacy programmes have been offered to vulnerable groups by nongovernmental organizations seeking to protect the interests of the groups. At present, literacy programmes need to be linked with health status, quality of life, and economic activity, to create an environment of success and capability.

General trends in mortality due to stomach, lung and cervical cancer

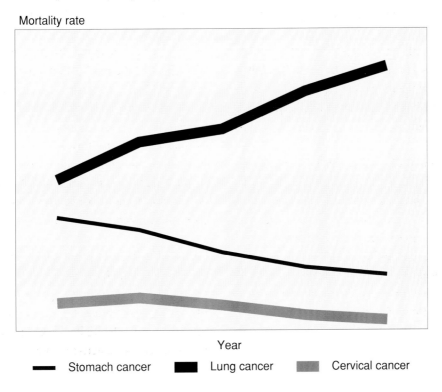

Mortality rate

Year

━━━ Stomach cancer   ▆ Lung cancer   ▨ Cervical cancer

Stomach cancer has been decreasing sharply and consistently in most areas. However, virtually all of the decline can be attributed to improvements in food preservation techniques and the resulting change in diet, rather than to any action of the medical community. The major exceptions to this decline are countries in Africa; this fact is consistent with the food-preservation and diet hypothesis.

Lung cancer mortality is rapidly increasing in most countries, especially in women. So far, only comprehensive tobacco control programmes in the United Kingdom and Finland have succeeded in reversing the upward trend in lung cancer mortality, and then only for males. It is clear that the fight against tobacco still has a long way to go. The general tendency, especially for females, is a marked increase in deaths from lung cancer.

Cervical cancer screening is considered responsible for most of the decline seen in cervical cancer mortality. A consistently clear association was seen in countries that had coordinated national programmes with high levels of coverage and well organized cytology laboratories. Changes in sexual behaviour may also have played an important role in cervical cancer trends.

Source: WHO.

A constant flow of the right kind of information helped consumers of industrialized nations confront the hazards of pollution and lifestyle with physical fitness and dietary changes.

"Eat well...live well"

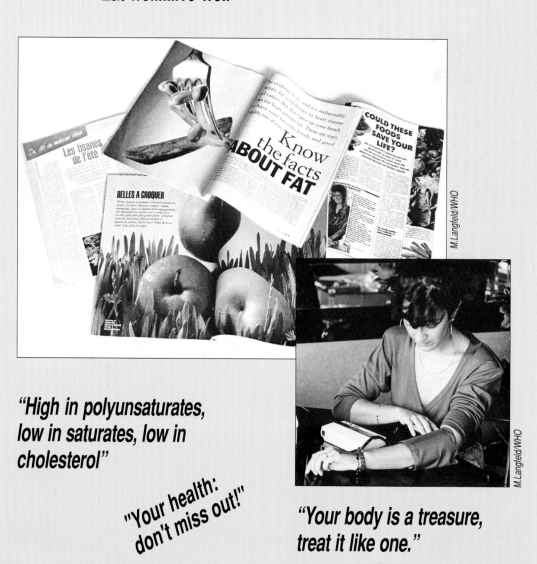

M.Langfeld/WHO

M.Langfeld/WHO

"High in polyunsaturates, low in saturates, low in cholesterol"

"Your health: don't miss out!"

"Your body is a treasure, treat it like one."

"Lifestyles influence health"

A UK Health Education Council poster

"Add life to years"

"Running puts you first in the race for a healthy life"

"Tobacco: how you can quit smoking!"

M.Langfeld/WHO

"Even a moderate increase in muscular activity contributes to better health."

Chapter 4
Linking economic well-being with health status

The economic cost of vulnerable and marginalized groups to society as a whole is high. There is the cost in terms of the unrealized productive potential of these groups; in poor countries they form a significant proportion of the work force, and their low productivity is a constraint on growth.

In addition, the AIDS pandemic has dramatically changed existing and future scenarios. The consequences on the economies of developing countries will be devastating because of the heavy toll that AIDS is taking on the labour force.

Well documented and accurate estimates of the size of the highly vulnerable groups are not available. But if broad estimates of the population below the poverty line in countries are used as an indication, the segment considered here lies between 30% and 40% of the population in the poorest countries. In countries where there are higher levels of per capita income, such as in Latin America, the same extremes of poverty may exist. In other countries, the economic elements of high vulnerability are related to unemployment, incapacity to engage in productive work, and economically marginalized conditions.

Table 6: **The economic burden of adult illness, selected countries and years**

	Days ill (past month)	Work days absent (past month)	Potential income loss (percentage of normal earnings)
Ghana, 1988/89	3.6	1.3	6.4
Côte d'Ivoire, 1987	2.6	1.3	6.4
Mauritania, 1988	2.1	1.6	6.5
Indonesia, 1978	1.0	0.6	2.5
Philippines (Bicol region), 1978	0.9	0.6	2.5
Bolivia (urban), 1990	—	1.2	4.4
Peru, 1985/86	4.5	0.9	3.1
Jamaica, 1989	1.2	0.5	2.1
United States, 1988	—	0.3	1.5

Note: Countries were selected on the basis of data availability.

a. To calculate these numbers for the eight developing countries, the probability of being ill (or absent from work) was multiplied by the number of days ill (or work days lost because of illness) in the month before the survey.
b. Potential income loss is the probable number of days of absence from work as a percentage of reported normal days at work.
c. For the United States, data are reported for the number of restricted-activity days resulting from illness in the population aged eighteen to forty-four years.

Sources: For the United States, U.S. Department of Health and Human Services 1989. For other countries, household surveys.
World Bank, *World Development Report 1991.*

Ill-health and economic retardation

Better health is desirable as an end in itself. But it also brings substantial economic benefits – releasing resources that can then be used to achieve other development goals. Better health and nutrition raise workers' productivity, decrease the number of days they are ill, and prolong their potential working lives. By reducing morbidity and debility, the malaria eradication programme in Sri Lanka in the 1940s and 1950s led to a 10% rise in incomes. In Sierra Leone, a 10% increase in the caloric intake of farm workers consuming 1500 calories a day raised output by 5%. Similar results have been found among Kenyan road construction workers with a daily intake of 2000 calories.

Household survey data from nine countries suggest that the economic effects of illness may be substantial. An average adult worker in Peru might expect to be ill 4.5 days a month and miss about one day of work as a result; in Ghana, the corresponding figures were 3.6 and 1.3 days (see table page 37). In the United States, workers aged between 18 and 44 years miss, on average, one-quarter of a day's work a month.

The potential income loss from illness in eight developing countries averages 2.1-6.5% of yearly earnings. Reducing illness obviously requires resources, but these figures suggest that it might yield a large benefit even in narrow economic terms, in addition to its human benefits.

Potential loss of earnings is only a partial measure of output loss. The full cost would include the value of lost nonmarket work (such as child care and food preparation), foregone earnings of other household members, costs of treatment, and so on. On the whole, the strictly economic case for effective efforts to improve health is strong.

Health and nutrition also have long-term effects on productivity and output because they influence a child's ability and motivation to learn. Among Nepalese children height-for-age, a measure of nutritional history, was found to be the most important factor, after family income, in explaining grade or school enrolment and attainment. In the Philippines, weight-for-height was a significant predictor of performance in mathematics achievement tests among urban schoolchildren. These effects, in turn, influence adult productivity. Studies in south India and the Philippines suggest that the long-term effects of nutrition on wages can be large and positive.

Source: World Bank, *World Development Report 1991.*

Another economic cost is that of state welfare programmes, services such as free or subsidized health care, and the income transfers of various kinds which are needed as some measure of relief and support to vulnerable groups while they continue in their deprived conditions.

In contrast to this welfare-oriented approach, in which a continuing financial burden is borne by the state, other strategies seek to enable vulnerable groups to contribute to a sustained process of economic growth by promoting their income-earning capacity. In such an approach the alleviation of vulnerability is market-oriented, involving a diminishing dependence on welfare and an increasing degree of self-reliance on the part of the vulnerable groups.

AIDS pandemic – some current and future dimensions

AIDS is a disease that kills people in their most productive years. At least half of those infected are under the age of 25.

The economic and social impact of AIDS will be immense. Its selective impact on young and middle-aged adults who include members of social, economic and political elites could lead to economic and even political destabilization in some countries severely affected by the disease.

HIV infection and its consequences are changing the world in which young people find themselves and rapidly altering the context in which they have to make decisions about behaviour.

■ As of April 1991, at least 8-10 million HIV infections are estimated to have occurred in adults worldwide, since the beginning of the pandemic. About one million children are estimated to have been born infected with HIV. For the year 2000 WHO's current global projection is that there will be a total of about 40 million HIV infections and 10 million AIDS cases.

■ By early 1991 an estimated 1.5 million HIV infections may have occurred in Australasia, North America and Western Europe, about two-thirds of these in the USA.

■ In many large cities in Australia, North America and Western Europe, AIDS has become a major cause of death in young adults aged 20-40 years. During the 1990s, HIV-related deaths will become one of the leading causes, if not the leading cause of death in this age group. As early as 1988 AIDS was the leading cause of death in both men and women aged 25-34 in New York City.

■ Estimates of total HIV infections are difficult to make for Latin America because of the relatively limited data available, but by early 1991 the cumulative total was estimated to be close to one million.

■ In sub-Saharan Africa, as of early 1991, the cumulative total in adults may be conservatively estimated at close to six million. In East and Central Africa, between one-quarter and one-third of all adults aged 15-49 living in some large urban centres had been infected with HIV by early 1991. It is estimated that about 900 000 HIV-infected infants will have been born in Africa by early 1991 and the projected total by the end of the 1990s is 10 million or more. It is estimated that more than 10 million children of less than 10 years of age in the region may be orphaned as a result of maternal AIDS during the 1990s .

■ In South and South-East Asia the pandemic is still at an early stage. There is concern that it is growing at a pace reminiscent of that in sub-Saharan Africa in the early 1980s but it may have an even greater potential for spread, given the much larger population.

■ For many countries the health and social support infrastructures that are available are quite inadequate to cope with the clinical burden of HIV-related disease. AIDS patients already comprise 20-40% of all hospitalized patients in Central and East Africa.

Source: Extracted from *Current and Future Dimensions of the HIV/AIDS Pandemic – A Capsule Summary.* Geneva, World Health Organization, 1991 (unpublished document WHO/GPA/RES/SFI/91.4).

People in poverty in developing countries

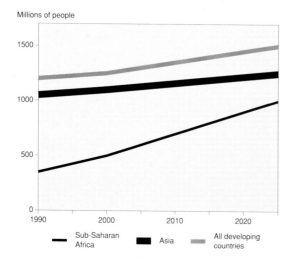

Millions of people

Legend:
- Sub-Saharan Africa
- Asia
- All developing countries

People in poverty in industrial countries

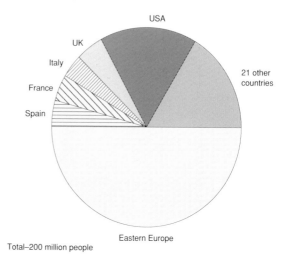

Total–200 million people

Source: UNDP, *Human Development Report*, 1991, p.26.

These strategies, which have been implemented primarily in developing countries, focus increasingly on designing and delivering lending, technology transfer, and other service "packages" that open up greater income-earning opportunities for the vulnerable groups, most of which are found in the unofficial sector, whether small-scale agriculture or elsewhere. The strategies assign high priority to micro-enterprises and various forms of self-employment. Economic activities have generally been based on assets already available to the household, such as small plots of farm land that could yield a higher income with an appropriate crop mixture and more intensive use, or on activity in the service sector, or on a new processing and manufacturing enterprise.

However, many obstacles remain that in themselves act as a deterrent in making the leap forward envisaged for the vulnerable groups. The groups are perceived as having a low level of creditworthiness because of their inability to satisfy conventional criteria for asset ownership

and income-earning capacity. Other aspects are low levels of functional literacy, the consequent lack of a basic capacity to acquire know-how and technology, and poor health status, all leading to low productivity and an inferior quality of life.

There are, however, numerous preconditions that have to be satisfied before vulnerable groups can be brought into such a process. Each of the elements in the package – access to income-earning assets and credit, technology, and extension services – has to be designed to meet the specific conditions of deprivation of the vulnerable groups involved. The success of the economic enterprises of the groups depends on overcoming all three constraints together. The five country projects in Africa for the highly vulnerable group of childbearing women attempted to do so. Conventional market lending, however, does not normally concern itself with an integrated programme within which the enterprise is itself located; its primary concern is the viability of the lending operation itself.

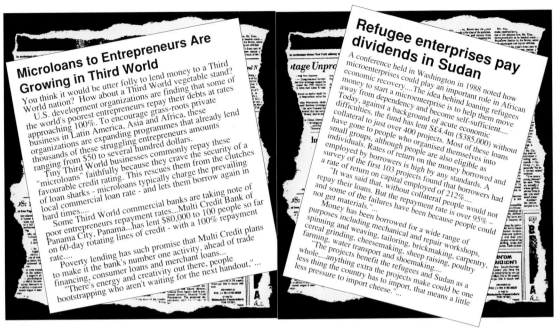

Microloans to Entrepreneurs Are Growing in Third World

You think it would be utter folly to lend money to a Third World nation? How about a Third World vegetable stand? U.S. development organizations are finding that some of the world's poorest entrepreneurs repay their debts at rates approaching 100%. To encourage grass-roots private business in Latin America, Asia and Africa, these organizations are expanding programmes that already lend thousands of these struggling entrepreneurs amounts ranging from $50 to several hundred dollars.

Tiny Third World businesses commonly repay these "microloans" faithfully because they crave the security of a favourable credit rating. This rescues them from the clutches of loan sharks - microloans typically charge the prevailing local commercial loan rate - and lets them borrow again in hard times....

Some Third World commercial banks are taking note of poor entrepreneurs repayment rates...Multi Credit Bank of Panama City, Panama...has lent $80,000 to 100 people so far on 60-day rotating lines of credit - with a 100% repayment rate....

Poverty lending has such promise that Multi Credit plans to make it the bank's number one activity, ahead of trade financing, consumer loans and merchant loans...

"There's energy and creativity out there, people bootstrapping who aren't waiting for the next handout," ...

Refugee enterprises pay dividends in Sudan

A conference held in Washington in 1988 noted how microenterprises could play an important role in African economic recovery....The idea behind loaning refugees money to start a microenterprise is to help them move away from dependency and become self-sufficient....

Today, against a background of acute economic difficulties, the fund has lent S£4.4m ($385,000) without collateral to just over 400 projects. Most of these loans have gone to people who organised themselves into small groups, although people are also eligible as individuals. Rates of return on the money borrowed and employed by borrowers is high by any standards. A survey of the first 103 projects found that borrowers had a rate of return on capital employed of 212%....

"It was said that, without collateral people would not repay their loans. But the repayment rate is over 95% – and some of the failures have been because people could not get materials,"...

Money has been borrowed for a wide range of purposes including mechanical and repair workshops, spinning and weaving, tailoring, brickmaking, carpentry, cereal grinding, cheesemaking, sheep raising, poultry farming, water transport and shoemaking....

"The projects benefit the refugees and Sudan as a whole....anything extra the projects make could be one less thing the country has to import, that means a little less pressure to import cheese." ...

New approaches to credit are extending opportunities to groups long denied access to loans. The next step is to link lending not only to greater income but also to better health.

Recent experience of programmes that have provided credit to vulnerable groups demonstrates that there are new innovative approaches to the problem of creditworthiness of vulnerable groups that have proved effective. Most of the successful programmes have adopted forms of group lending that have been able to overcome the problems of use and repayment and make the lending operation viable with market interest rates and relatively low servicing costs.

Market rates have not imposed an excessive burden on borrowers, who were paying much higher rates in the unofficial sector. Contrary to popular belief, borrowers under these programmes, who are often among the poorest of the poor, have had impressive records of repayment, sometimes doing better than those in conventional lending programmes. Servicing costs have been kept low through the sharing of responsibility between the lending institution and the group. Devices such as small initial short-term loans with the prospect of re-lending have tested the creditworthiness of borrowers

and consolidated relationships between the borrower and the lending institution.

The vulnerable groups have also demonstrated the capacity to maximize the returns from the money they borrow. Given access to the resources needed, they can soon increase their income-earning capacity and become increasingly self-reliant. For example, in a small-scale enterprise credit scheme in Calcutta, with approximately 30 000 clients, the average income of borrowers increased by approximately 80%. In the Kupedes programme in Indonesia, with nearly 1.3 million borrowers, the income of the average borrower rose by about 150% in three years. These examples illustrate another very important feature of the growth that comes from alleviation of the poverty of and investment by the vulnerable groups – there is a high output per unit of investment and a low capital-output ratio.

However, the strategies that are being evolved for alleviation of poverty have seldom been

Creative credit: selected examples

Credit and savings programmes that have successfully assisted vulnerable groups have been placed in four categories: commercial banks; intermediaries that facilitate links between commercial banks and borrowers; parallel programmes, usually of NGOs that obtain alternative sources of funds and provide loans directly; and poverty-oriented development banks that have a more assured formal structure. Innovative activities have been initiated by institutions in each category.

For example, in Indonesia the KUPEDES and SIMPEDES programmes of the Government's Bank Rakyat have targeted micro-entrepreneurs, 25% of loans going to women. KUPEDES provides credit and SIMPEDES stimulates savings. The programmes are also profitable for the Government – KUPEDES' net income alone in 1989 was over US$ 20 million and the system is now self-financing. Because they are built into a massive banking system, they can reach large numbers of borrowers throughout the country. Successful rural development or micro-entrepreneurial funds have been initiated by commercial and government banks in a number of other countries, including Ecuador, Nepal and Peru. In the United States the South Shore Bank has made profits of US$1.5 million as a result of lending to small-scale enterprises in some of the poorest areas of Chicago.

ACCION International, an intermediary organization, represents a network of 50 affiliates working in 12 countries in Latin America and the Caribbean and serves over 50 000 borrowers organized in solidarity groups. ACCION's major activity is the provision of market-rate loans and training in business skills for low-income micro-entrepreneurs. In 1990 its total lending amounted to about US$ 37.8 million. Through the development of guarantee funds for its affiliates, ACCION has convinced numerous private banks in the region that it is sound policy to lend to micro-entrepreneurs. It is no longer solely reliant on contributions, interest, or fees for its capital. Several years ago ACCION began buying letters of credit in commercial money markets and making them available to its affiliates, thereby greatly expanding the number of loans that could be offered.

The Grameen Bank is perhaps the most famous poverty-oriented development bank. Another is the Badan Kredit Kecamatan (BKK), which establishes sub-district financial boards to stimulate savings and to disburse small loans. About a third of all loans go to individuals, mainly women, and no collateral is required, but a commercial rate of interest is charged. The capital for loans is largely derived from deposit savings. BKK reached approximately 2.7 million people in 1982. The key to BKK's success includes

- the support of government and of its operation in financial institutions
- serving areas that no other financial institutions serve
- using the influence and guidance of village leaders through the formation of decentralized credit committees, to ensure that borrowers are creditworthy.

A fifth group, local rotating savings and credit associations, is becoming of increasing importance. Small self-formed groups of poor women or men have traditionally joined together in villages in many countries for the express purpose of quickly generating savings funds and establishing longer-term emergency funds. These associations include tontines in Cameroon, arisans in Indonesia, otu-otu contribution clubs in western Nigeria, susus in Ghana and Kenya, and many others. Today many of these groups are formal structures with access to commercial banks or government credit sources.

In the Sarvodaya Credit Scheme in Sri Lanka, the Sarvodaya centre in the village initiates the formation of village societies of mixed male and female groups. Societies go through a rigorous training period during which time each member enters a compulsory savings scheme. Such savings act as collateral for loans. The Sarvodaya thereafter lends a sum of money to the society and the society in turn lends to members, the amount lent varying according to the project the member presents. The society charges an interest of 20% per annum on the loan. It repays Sarvodaya at 15% per annum.

Sources include: Holt, S.L. & Ribe, H., *Developing financial institutions for the poor and reducing barriers to access for women*, World Bank Discussion Paper No. 117, 1991; Sarvodaya Economic Enterprises Development Services (SEEDS), Accounts and progress report for 12 months from 1st April 1990 to 31st March 1991. Prepared by Sarvodaya Economic Enterprises Development Services, March 1991.

A small loan leads to big benefits

Mrs Manowara's history is similar to that of many women who have benefited from Grameen bank loans. The poverty of her family forced her to drop out of school in her third year. Her first husband divorced her because her family could not provide a dowry, and her second husband was too old to do farm labour, so the family had no income.

Through a village bank worker she learned about the Grameen Bank's activities and was able to form a group with four other women. Each member of the group contributed one taka a week for seven weeks to a group savings fund prior to making a request to the bank for loans.

Mrs Manowara was the fifth in line to receive a loan. With her first 2000 taka she invested in stocks of basic staple foods to sell to her neighbours. While she was able to repay the initial loan instalments, she found it difficult to save, so with subsequent loans she decided to invest progressively in more lucrative enterprises. With her third loan of 2500 taka she purchased used garments in another village market which she then sold at a profit in her own village. Further loans were then used to expand her business.

With five years of assistance from the bank, Mrs Manowara can meet her family's basic needs. An 8000 taka loan from the bank made it possible for her, with her family and her group members' help, to construct a new clay-walled, tin-roofed home and a model latrine. She has enough food to feed her family, and her children are able to attend school. She has chickens and fruit trees, and she grows vegetables, jute and paddy to supplement her income and cover the cost of medicine, clothing, festival expenses, and entertainment.

Source: International Dialogue and Exposure Programme, jointly organized by the German Commission for Justice and Peace and the Grameen Bank, Bangladesh, 14-22 October 1989.

concerned directly with the link between the economic component and health status. Increase in income by itself will not ensure that these groups use the income to improve their health status and quality of life. Increased income can be used in the adoption of patterns of consumption and lifestyles injurious to health and so produce health hazards that did not exist earlier. Economic motivation may inculcate values encouraging short-term material gain at the expense of health and quality of life.

This can be avoided and the process of change managed in an orderly way if health criteria and objectives form part of the economic decision-making of the households from the beginning. The key question, however, is whether it is possible to incorporate them directly into the process of lending itself. The most effective way of doing so is to insert a health condition into the lending operation, thereby linking both economic and health objectives.

There is a wide range of options that can be considered in attempting to make health a condition of lending. One is in relation to the health hazards of the project for individuals and the community. Lending institutions could take into account the health impact of the project they finance and avoid lending for projects that are injurious to health. The borrower and the health authorities would be jointly responsible for studying the risks involved as well as the measures proposed to overcome them.

Most of the conditions governing such aspects already exist. To make them operational, regulations would have to be imposed and banks obliged to take the health aspect into account in their lending. The regulations would

Drugs, Suburban Violence, Fundamentalism

Drugs, violence in the suburbs, the growth of fundamentalism ... when these apparently unconnected phenomena occur everywhere at the same time, it is not by chance. Between them and the spirit of the age there must be some link....

As for the economy, when living standards were close to subsistence level and production activities were essentially agricultural, any increase in production led to an improvement in well-being. Quantity meant quality....

On the other hand, when the impact of production activities damages and threatens to destroy the mechanisms that regulate the biosphere, we can no longer evade the question of sustainable development and the rights of future generations on this planet, which we imagine we are bequeathing to them whereas we are really borrowing it from them....

Insidiously, over the years, in the parts of the world where liberalism prevailed just as in those that claimed to be socialist, the emphasis laid on income and on ways of obtaining a better life has ultimately eclipsed the objectives these systems are supposed to serve. For lack of true ideals, we resort to market regulation, competition, money....

have to have effect in ways similar to those concerning the environment and be enforced similarly. Many countries already have the legal framework for such regulations. Under such a system, the lending institution would have little more to do than verify that the enterprise had been properly registered and cleared from the health standpoint. The procedure would be similar to that of a bank making a housing loan for a building approved by a local authority on a plan satisfying stipulated health criteria, or of a micro-enterprise given clearance in relation to its environmental impact.

A regulatory framework of this kind would have to avoid the development of a bureaucratic machinery with the risk of becoming cumbersome and posing a serious constraint to the development of economic enterprises. An effective system could, however, be developed that took known health effects into account prior to approval of a project.

Another option is somewhat more complicated. It could include the positive impact of economic activities on the health of individuals and the community. It could cover a tax payment to a special fund set up by the community for a fresh water supply, drainage, or a waste collection system. It could be extended to programmes dealing with health hazards such as alcohol, drugs, tobacco, and family planning.

Other options relate to conditions of eligibility at the time of borrowing or to future behaviour and action on the part of the borrower. Options for conditionality could include participation in health programmes such as family planning or immunization. There are, however, problems in giving effect to such conditions and making them operational. Lending institutions, for example, might regard the conditions as extraneous to their lending operations and primary financial objectives, and the conditions would add to their work and might affect adversely

Preventing health hazards in micro-enterprises

As governments turn to the informal work sector to increase employment opportunities, attention should be given to the measures to be taken to reduce related health risks and apply health conditionality. The risks are real, as the following example shows:

Twenty-two children in Kingston, Jamaica, were hospitalized for lead poisoning between January 1986 and March 1987. The effects were found to vary with the quantities of lead present, but included damage to the kidney, liver, nervous system, and reproductive system. In addition, growth was impaired and blood synthesis interfered with. An epidemiological investigation revealed that the most likely source of exposure was ingestion of contaminated soil. Soil contamination resulted from lead fumes generated during work in a local repair shop or smelting of scrap lead, lead dust blown from piles of scrap, from scrap dragged or carted through yards, or from lead dust adhering to the shoes of workers. Examination of blood from different groups found the highest blood lead levels in children under five years of age living close to the repair shop.

Such situations are difficult to control, especially when there are many establishments and each one is small. Few, if any, developing countries have the capacity to carry out the necessary field visits and tests to ensure the safety of such establishments. A more effective strategy would involve incorporating protective measures from the beginning. For example, when such enterprises seek initial capital funding, the local entrepreneurs can be informed of associated health risks and of steps to mitigate such risks. Ideally, these steps would be built into the financial support terms, for example in the detailed specification of the manufacturing and testing equipment to be used. Once such equipment had been purchased, it would be in the interest of the establishment to ensure that it was used correctly and that risks were minimized. The government's role would be to identify the situations of greatest public health risk and provide information on their reduction in a form usable by local banks.

Source: Matte, T.D. et al. Lead poisoning among household members exposed to lead-acid battery repair shops in Kingston, Jamaica. *International Journal of Epidemiology*, 18: 874-81 (1989).

their relationship with customers, which both parties would prefer to maintain on exclusively financial terms.

Even if such conditions were included and even if they were as specific as participation in a family planning or immunization programme, lending institutions might not be willing to undertake the task of monitoring their fulfilment. Either the lending institutions would have to undertake such a task as a social responsibility or they would have to be persuaded that it was in their financial interests to do so.

Lending institutions could be encouraged to include a simple list of health criteria and health risks that would be taken into account in assessing the risks involved in lending to any given borrower. This however must not operate in a manner that placed further constraints on vulnerable groups in obtaining loans. It would have to relate to action that is already taken or would be taken to protect and safeguard health.

There are special reasons why the health status of vulnerable groups is of crucial importance. A serious illness, a death in the family, or a birth

---

Health as a community priority

The Grameen Bank, in addition to individual loans for economic activities, also provides loans to groups for collective enterprises. Such joint loans have been given for over 100 different activities and by June 1991, 126.6 million taka (US$ 3.52 million) had been disbursed to fund them. These include the purchase of shallow tubewells, deep tubewells, and rice and oil mills, the leasing of markets, ponds, and land, and the purchase of power tillers, wheat threshers, etc.

It would be possible to build on this procedure and take it one step further by linking group loans to improved health status and quality of life. For example, a financial institution could make available a group health savings account which would receive a higher rate of interest, similar to that of term deposits, with the understanding that the capital and interest accrued would be used for collective activities directly related to the promotion of health and well-being in the community. Such activities might include combating malaria in an infested area by filling swamps, clearing weeds, or buying mosquito netting for all members of the community. Other infrastructural activities might be investment in boreholes, covering existing open wells, or constructing latrines or health posts.

Collective activities to promote health and well-being in the community could be profit-making ventures in themselves. In this way members of the group with the group health savings account could be shareholders and expect dividends from profit-making enterprises such as village pharmacies, local shops stocking essential commodities, and community farms. Decisions would be taken by the group on the level of savings required by each member, the use of money, and dividend payments.

Part of the group health savings account might also be set aside as collective social security to cover situations such as community care facilities for AIDS patients and emergency relief and reconstruction for natural disasters such as floods and cyclones.

Source: Unpublished report of Steering Committee meeting for International Forum, WHO, Geneva, Switzerland, 29–31 July 1991.

---

can impose a severe financial strain on their meagre budget. It can therefore be argued that whatever protective action can be taken to minimize health hazards becomes important in lending to vulnerable groups. The inclusion of health criteria in the assessment of the risks of lending would have an impact on both lender and borrower and increase public awareness of health status as an element that must be taken into account in economic decision-making.

The assumption that lending institutions would assent to bringing health considerations into lending itself rests on the expectation that they would be ready to overcome the barriers created by the vulnerable condition of the groups. The task would be much easier for lending institutions and credit schemes specifically concerned with vulnerable groups and readier to view lending in relation to the total vulnerability of the borrowers.

The approaches discussed raise a number of wide-ranging issues regarding the role of the market in the economic transformation of vulnerable groups. The main thrust of the strategy must no doubt be market-based if it is to be sustainable. Transformation implies

---

Health and individual savings and loans

An increase in income does not necessarily lead to an improvement in health status. Many studies have shown that women are more likely than men to use their own earnings on food and other essential goods for the family, but this is not always the case.

Just as certain economic conditions such as interest rates, collaterals, and repayment periods are conditions for obtaining individual loans, so too health status and quality of life can be made part of the loan process, the specific health conditions, hazards, and risks of the borrower and the community being assessed at the time of the application for the loan. The candidate would be required to open an individual health savings account with the financial institution, and a portion of the increased income generated from the economic activity as a result of the loan would be paid weekly or monthly into the account. The savings would then be used to deal with the priority health problems identified, thus improving the borrower's health credit rating and qualifying the individual borrower or the group for future loans at preferential rates of interest or for other incentives.

The health savings account might be used for the purchase of nutritious foods to combat malnutrition, for treatment of alcoholism or drug addiction, or for buying thermometers to use when fever is suspected. It could also be used as a personal health insurance to pay for unforeseen medical costs or as buffer savings to tide AIDS victims over times of illness when they are unable to work.

Source: Unpublished report of Steering Committee meeting for International Forum, WHO, Geneva, Switzerland, 29–31 July 1991.

---

capacity to compete efficiently in the market. The elements described – borrowing techniques, market interest rates for lending, economic viability of the micro-enterprises – would permit the strategy to become part of a larger strategy of development, using the market as the main instrument.

However, it would be wrong to conclude from this that market forces left entirely to themselves would be capable of generating the entire process. Many of the successes referred to required the support of NGOs, which did not have profit-making objectives as commercial banks have. Non-profit institutions at the apex and value systems oriented towards social objectives were an essential part of the success-ful programme. In many instances the servicing costs were not borne entirely by the borrower.

The catalytic role these institutions played was indispensable for the entire operation.

It is doubtful whether the servicing costs, including the cost of the infrastructure providing the supportive services described, can be transferred entirely to the borrower or the micro-enterprise, even if part of the initial cost of project preparation and servicing could be built into the loan; a substantial component would have to be financed out of resources mobilized by the state and the NGOs. It would be difficult to conceive of a strategy that would rapidly transform the vulnerable groups, unless it was underpinned by the value systems that motivate the NGOs and had an adequate element of assistance for the development of the infra-structure.

Health as a condition for credit and savings: the first steps

In the five country projects, small but significant steps have been taken both to improve the overall access of vulnerable groups to financial services and to design schemes that place emphasis on simultaneous improvement in health and economic status as an essential condition of credit operations. An example of this is the Ghana rural credit scheme for women.

This scheme represents the culmination of efforts to introduce a real grass-roots, beneficiary-participatory, cost-effective credit scheme that suits the present situation of vulnerable women. Under the scheme, the project provides small short-term loans to poor women for economic activities of their choice in which they are already experienced, and for which markets and the required inputs are available locally.

The loans are given to individual women borrowers who organize themselves first into small mutual guarantee groups designated as solidarity groups (SGs). The solidarity group consists of 4-7 individuals who know each other well and have agreed to be guarantors for each other in obtaining a loan from the project. Members have a primary responsibility to help one another in their choice of income-generating activities and in any circumstances that might make it impossible for a member to make repayments as they become due. In case of default on the part of an individual, it is the responsibility of the other members of the solidarity group to which the defaulter belongs to repay to the project the loan advanced to the defaulter as well as the added interest.

These solidarity groups are further grouped into community credit committees (CCCs). The CCCs are independent entities trained and sponsored by the project to receive, manage and repay loans, subject to the requirements of the project. Each CCC creates its own procedures for loans, within the rules set by the project for eligibility as a CCC. These rules ensure access to credit by the target beneficiaries, encourage borrower and CCC discipline, and protect the project's loan guarantee fund from decapitalization.

Another role of the CCCs is to collaborate with the participating sector agencies in the project to develop individual profiles of group members. Monitoring indicators are chosen which show change in the situation and health status of borrowers and this forms the basis for the monitoring and information system of the project, which will be shared by all interested parties including the beneficiaries themselves.

Non-literate members will initially be specially assisted through the use of pictorial charts to participate fully in the monitoring of their own progress, while the Non-formal Education Division of the Ministry of Education makes efforts to improve their literacy level.

The source of funding for the credit scheme is a revolving loan fund with inputs from donors. All loans given under the project have an interest rate of 20% per annum. The CCCs impose a levy upon borrowers which is not allowed to exceed 5% of the loan and is payable at the disbursement of the loan. This levy provides the CCC with its initial working capital.

As each CCC accumulates its own funds in the form of fees, savings, and levies on members, it has a free hand to invest them as the members wish. The CCC is expected gradually to become eligible to receive loans from banks without third party guarantees. The CCC may eventually accumulate enough funds to provide its members with adequate credit without recourse to project or bank loans.

Other benefits of the credit scheme include:
- weekly meetings where beneficiaries come together to increase their resources through loan repayments and savings, obtain useful information and consider more effective ways of using available resources,
- training programmes,
- incentives for regular savings.

Source: Documents from project "Improving Health through Women's Functional Literacy and Intersectoral Action", Ghana, 1991.

It will be difficult to adapt the existing institutional framework for market lending to all the tasks that have been outlined, without special incentives and resources earmarked for the purpose. The institutions now operating that have developed some capacity for innovative forms of lending to vulnerable groups, such as the Grameen Bank, the small-scale enterprise credit scheme in Calcutta, and the Badan Kredit Kecamatan of Indonesia, have been functioning outside mainstream market lending. Any expansion of their initiatives and any attempt to bring the mainstream lending institutions into the strategy for taking the vulnerable groups out of their present condition would require an effort on a larger scale.

One possibility would be a separate financing institution operating at the international level and playing a catalytic role in introducing market disciplines into lending operations. Such an institution should be able to increase the flow of credit for financing the micro-enterprises of vulnerable groups and in doing so ensure that the health component is incorporated into the arrangements for loans.

There are various organizational options for such an institution. It could function as a major non-profit NGO or foundation now functions and work through a network of credit institutions already operating at the national level. It could be established in the form of a social development bank promoting the establishment of counterparts at the national level, as for example the Janasaviya Trust in Sri Lanka, and acting through them. It could also operate as a refinancing facility to banks to enable them to increase their credit to vulnerable groups and, in doing so, incorporate health objectives in their lending.

These alternatives need not be mutually exclusive. They could be combined in a single institution designed to play the catalytic role envisaged.

The delta system

The delta system, on the basis of its ability to raise capital, provides capital to institutions below the market rate. This is done by issuing and insuring commercial paper and charging transaction fees. The local association, bank, or credit union makes loans at reduced rates of interest for economically viable projects, making improved health status a condition of the loans.

Source: Unpublished report of Steering Committee meeting for International Forum, WHO, Alexandria, Egypt, 11–14 June 1991.

The Janasaviya Trust – credit fund in Sri Lanka

The credit fund facilitates access to credit for intermediaries who provide loans to the poor and unemployed for micro-enterprise development and self-employment.

NGOs, grass-roots organizations, government programmes and cooperative and financial intermediaries that lend to the poor, meet specific financial and programme criteria, and enter into participation agreements with the Fund, are eligible for financing as partner organizations (POs).

To be a PO, an organization must have at least two years' experience in lending to the target population. The loan recovery rate for the two years preceding a loan application to the Fund must be at least 70%.

The applying organization must have a credit methodology permitting small short-term loans at commercial rates after three months of participatory training or mobilization activity, rely on character references rather than asset collateral, and use repeat loans as an incentive for full and timely repayment.

To be eligible for continued financing from the Fund, the loan recovery rate of the PO must be at least 90% for lent funds. The sub-borrowers must be the poor, women, and unemployed youth. The objective of the Fund should be to make 40-50% of the loans to women.

The sub-borrowers must be the poor as defined by the Trust, organized in a group for the purpose of borrowing and actively participating in a savings programme. Lending is for productive micro-enterprise development and self-employment, not for consumption. Lending terms are short and typically do not exceed 12 months. Loans to first-time borrowers are small and should not exceed Rs 20 000 (c. US $ 500). Interest rates are commercial, covering the PO's operation and risk costs. The minimum rate is 1% above the weighted average commercial bank lending rate.

Interest rates charged to POs by the credit fund should allow POs an adequate margin to cover lending cost and risks; at minimum not less than 7%. Trust financing in general should not exceed 20% of the PO's existing portfolio.

Source: Janasaviya Trust Fund. Programme Policy Manual, Operations Manual, 1990. Unpublished working document for Janasaviya Trust Fund officials.

Chapter 5
Beyond the welfare-oriented approach

The major focus of the approach described here is on the transformation of vulnerable and marginalized groups into productive self-reliant partners in the social and economic development of their countries. It rests on the capacity to strengthen vulnerable groups in such a way that they themselves become responsible for promoting and improving their health status and quality of life as well as their economic productivity. This approach differs fundamentally from one that relies exclusively on state intervention and welfare for the relief of vulnerability through social security measures, subsidies, and income transfer.

Transforming the conditions of vulnerable groups and enhancing their self-reliance requires parallel interventions at the macro level that will create enabling conditions for the self-help efforts of the groups at the micro level and constantly make the necessary structural adjustments to support them.

For instance, it may be necessary to reform laws and create or strengthen institutions. The transformation of the vulnerable groups will in many cases require a re-ordering of the priorities of public investment policy so that adequate investment is made in the social and economic

Workfare Found to Save Money, Not Ease Poverty

"There is strong evidence that (mandatory work programs) worked. They got people off welfare and they were a good investment of taxpayer dollars," said Judith M. Gueron, the study's senior author. "But few of the programs ... moved families out of poverty and got people higher earnings and somewhat higher income....

Generally, (the study) shows these programs give us a realistic expectation that you can reduce welfare dependency, you can get people working but it is unlikely that with these programmes alone they can work their way out of poverty," ... Gueron said.

Because most of the early programmes were low cost and limited in their scope, the study said, they had two significant failings – they did not make much improvement in welfare recipients' standard of living and they did not reach long-term recipients who are the greatest burden to the welfare system....

infrastructure for the environment of the groups. In most developing countries this would mean the reorientation of trends and policies that have a pronounced urban bias and substantial outlays on health and educational services, roads, and transport and communication facilities. Above all, the banking and financial systems would have to support the vulnerable groups in their efforts to improve their income-earning capacity.

Market forces condition the choices of consumers with far-reaching consequences for their health as well as for that of future generations.

To manage the "health market" in a manner that gives due priority to health, society needs to strengthen existing mechanisms and develop new mechanisms that will effectively deal with the problems. First, there has to be a regular monitoring of the health status of the population and identification of the changing profile of vulnerability. Second, there has to be a continuous flow of information about the health consequences of developments and changes, as well as the policies that are being implemented. Third, there must be a regular opportunity for the public to express concerns about health and participate in discussion and action for its improvement. These are the essential elements in a strategy in which health becomes an integral part of development.

Analogy with the environment

Today the effect of development on the environment has become a central concern, both globally and nationally. For this to happen, environmental stress had to reach a point where it was perceived as approaching the limits of sustainability. On the other hand, the effect of development on health still remains secondary to most other development concerns. The tendency has been to approach it as a part of

New market forces in developing countries could jeopardize health

other issues as, for example, the health effects of development as byproducts of environmental degradation, or of poor health as an indicator of poverty. In these issues health still remains instrumental, a means to another development objective. As such it is undoubtedly important and necessary. But it is when health is valued for itself as an indispensable part of the quality of life, to be achieved through the processes of development, that it assumes its true role in development and the other sectoral objectives become aligned to essential health goals.

Awareness that health status has to be examined independently as a changing outcome of development has not yet adequately permeated development planning and policy-making. Knowledge of disease and technical ability to control it continue to advance, but changes in society that accompany changing patterns of production and consumption result in the slow accumulation of new health hazards and persistence and exacerbation of some of the hazards already existing. This is manifest in the

Consumption of alcoholic drinks by young men and young women

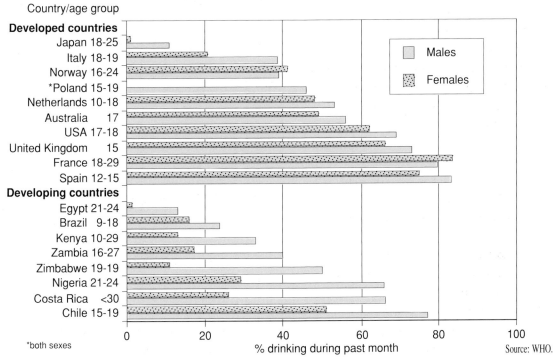

Country/age group

*both sexes

Worldwide consumption of alcoholic drinks by young people and adults has been increasing.

Drug-related deaths of young people, aged 10-24 years, Australia, 1985

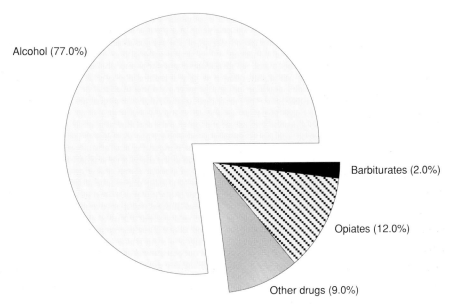

Alcohol (77.0%)

Barbiturates (2.0%)

Opiates (12.0%)

Other drugs (9.0%)

Source: WHO.

Alcohol-related mortality rates among all age groups, including the young, are a cause for concern.

conditions of high vulnerability that can be identified in all parts of the globe.

In the case of the environment, success in controlling nature and changing the ecosystem in the pursuit of production and consumption goals was valued over a long period as a positive indicator of development. Long-term environmental degradation was neglected until it had severely impaired the quality of life and begun to threaten the foundations of development itself. Such a fate can be avoided in the case of health only if the centrality of health in

development is recognized and the health goal given an equal place with the other important goals of development. This requires much more direct concern with the health outcomes of development than exists at present. Action has to be taken at the national and global level such as that at present being taken for the environment and development. Changes in the profiles of vulnerability would have to be used as indispensable measurements of the quality of life, and development strategies and policies would have to be constantly evaluated and adjusted accordingly.

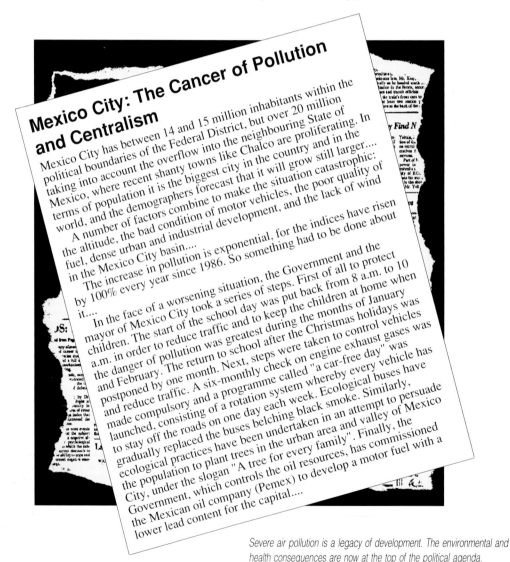

Mexico City: The Cancer of Pollution and Centralism

Mexico City has between 14 and 15 million inhabitants within the political boundaries of the Federal District, but over 20 million taking into account the overflow into the neighbouring State of Mexico, where recent shanty towns like Chalco are proliferating. In terms of population it is the biggest city in the country and in the world, and the demographers forecast that it will grow still larger....

A number of factors combine to make the situation catastrophic: the altitude, the bad condition of motor vehicles, the poor quality of fuel, dense urban and industrial development, and the lack of wind in the Mexico City basin....

The increase in pollution is exponential, for the indices have risen by 100% every year since 1986. So something had to be done about it....

In the face of a worsening situation, the Government and the mayor of Mexico City took a series of steps. First of all to protect children. The start of the school day was put back from 8 a.m. to 10 a.m. in order to reduce traffic and to keep the children at home when the danger of pollution was greatest during the months of January and February. The return to school after the Christmas holidays was postponed by one month. Next, steps were taken to control vehicles and reduce traffic. A six-monthly check on engine exhaust gases was made compulsory, and a programme called "a car-free day" was launched, consisting of a rotation system whereby every vehicle has to stay off the roads on one day each week. Ecological buses have gradually replaced the buses belching black smoke. Similarly, ecological practices have been undertaken in an attempt to persuade the population to plant trees in the urban area and valley of Mexico City, under the slogan "A tree for every family". Finally, the Government, which controls the oil resources, has commissioned the Mexican oil company (Pemex) to develop a motor fuel with a lower lead content for the capital....

Severe air pollution is a legacy of development. The environmental and health consequences are now at the top of the political agenda.

Examples of industrial and health goals striking the right balance

Naming 'Eco-Managers', German Firms Go Green

...But times are changing rapidly. As in much of the industrialized world, public awareness in Germany of ecological issues and matters of personal health is growing steadily, and it is affecting consumers' buying habits.

Companies are devoting increasing amounts of time, money and effort to developing products that are environmentally safe, promoting the benign nature of existing ones and presenting their environmental-protection policies in the best light....

Germany's vast chemical industry is at the forefront of the new environmental thinking.... environmental consciousness must become ingrained in managers' minds so that it is automatically part of the corporate decision-making process ... in a case where there is any doubt about the environmental impact, ... environmental protection comes before profits...

Better nutrition for Soviet workers:
The Elektrostal project

The problems of nutrition are identical in almost all developed countries, and the USSR is no exception. Excessive consumption of animal fats, salt and sugar, and insufficient consumption of fruit and vegetables, together with a lack of physical activity, increase the risk of noncommunicable diseases,...

...people are generally well informed about what healthy nutrition is, about the food products they should consume, and about what the necessary amounts and combinations are. But they cannot follow these requirements because of lack of available food, family traditions, lack of time, high prices and so on....

It has proved possible to arrange this in the context of large working collectives, such as the Elektrostal factory, provided the improvement of nutrition is directly linked with the correction of unhealthy habits and traditions....

Under market conditions, enterprises have to concern themselves with complex and long-term health promotion for their workers in order to reduce the loss of man-hours from illness and disability, and to increase the stability of the company....

Cleaner air at 10 000 metres
A smooth ride and passenger approval for the clean-air policy of airlines.

Will the 1990s see a worldwide ban on all smoking aboard airliners, however long or short the flight? A trend in that direction is already well under way....

One by one, the world's airlines are finding it both healthy and expedient to ban smoking from the passenger cabin... As one executive of a major airline commented frankly: "Although we will invariably lose some customers who prefer to smoke on flights, we are confident we will gain more new ones who prefer a healthy cabin environment."

International Labour Office

Managing the trade-offs between health and development

When the health goals of development are affirmed in this manner, the unavoidable trade-offs between health and the other sectoral goals can be achieved with the right balance.

Costs in terms of health and quality of life have been treated differently in different development strategies, depending on the relative importance assigned to the different goals. If the strategy is aimed at optimizing growth to the neglect of other development goals, it will be prepared to incur high health costs to lower the economic costs of production, in the hope that higher growth and greater economic resources will be able to deal at a later stage with the health problems that have emerged.

The assumptions underlying such a strategy are, however, often falsified, for a variety of reasons. The strategy ends up by building incentives, motivations, and values into the system in a manner that perpetuates the trade-offs. The life-styles and patterns of behaviour that evolve become entrenched and make it difficult to reverse the process. This has been the experience with trade-offs in the case of the environment.

On the other hand, if the strategy is based on achieving an equilibrium between the different development goals, on the assumption that each has its own independent value and is also essential for achieving the other, the allocation of resources and determination of priorities are fundamentally different. They are then governed by constant evaluation of the impact of any given set of policies and strategies on each of the development goals. Decisions are taken on assessments of the overall balance of costs and gains, both short-term and long-term.

Examples of this are the tobacco industry and the livestock industry. Strategies to align these industries to health goals are likely to have adverse economic consequences in the short term on specific groups, and in turn have health impacts. These would have to be compensated for as far as possible through the adoption of economic policies that would not jeopardize the final health goals, which remain paramount.

Some such situations may permit policies where the trade-offs could be phased and the health goal fully achieved over a period of time through the management of market forces. Others, such as narcotics, industrial safety, or pollution, may not be amenable to any health trade-off at all and health may need to be protected by much more direct intervention and conscious decision to bear all the economic costs involved.

Yet another type of trade-off would be that made in the case of a major hydroelectric or irrigation project with the potential to generate new health hazards on a large scale. Here the economic goals may take first place, but the potential health hazards would be identified and preventive action taken to minimize the health costs.

The scale and intensity of the health hazards, the threshold limits, and the time taken to reach those limits will vary in each situation and influence the final decisions on trade-offs. What is important, however, is that every such choice should be made within a framework in which health status is an integral part of development and cannot be traded off for any other element on a permanent or long-term basis. A full account of all short-term losses and trade-offs would have to be maintained. These losses and trade-offs must be constantly kept in view by development planners and policy makers and compensated within the shortest possible time so that the constant aim of development is the protection and enhancement of the total well-being of society.

Chapter 6
Health as conditionality for development

Definition and usage of the term conditionality

The term "conditionality" is generally used in connection with the dealings international financing institutions have with their member countries. It normally refers to a set of basic policy conditions that countries are required to fulfil and the adjustments they must undertake to become eligible for loans and financial assistance. In this publication the term is used in a more inclusive sense. First, it implies that the protection and improvement of health are a condition of development, and in this sense it refers to the health goals and health constraints that must be taken into account in development policies. Second, it denotes the conditions and criteria relating to health applied by governments in the allocation of budgetary resources to various sectors. Third, it refers to the conditions attached to loans and development assistance by international financing institutions and banks in the country.

Identifying the elements of health-related conditionality

At the macro level, integration of the main health goals in overall development goals is a complex task. The basic elements of the process are not fundamentally different from those involved in the setting of macroeconomic goals and the formulation of strategies for achieving them. First, how should the main health goals themselves be defined and the targets set as for the macroeconomic targets of growth, income, and employment? Second, are there key policy instruments or is there a set of macro policies that have to be carried out as for the implementation of policies relating to the government budget, the balance of payments, and the money supply? Macroeconomic conditionality for development is defined in terms of such parameters. What are the basic parameters in the case of health?

Some of the problems related to this issue are reflected in the recent experience of countries in attempting to deal with the adverse social impacts of structural adjustment. A typical response has been to design special programmes that provide some measure of relief to vulnerable groups that have been affected. Some well-designed programmes include special employment-generating projects, public works programmes, and interventions in the fields of health, nutrition and education. There is no doubt that social action programmes of this nature have fulfilled an urgent need to compensate for the adverse social outcomes of economic adjustment policies. To the extent that they have now become a regular concomitant of the measures taken, they indicate an important modification in the strategies of structural adjustment: policy-makers concerned exclusively with macroeconomic adjustments have recognized the adverse social effects of those adjustments and the need to intervene to mitigate them. However, the interventions have been designed essentially as remedial and compensatory measures, the implicit assumption being that the adverse effects are inevitable and that economic adjustments will lead to economic growth that will then also promote a positive social outcome. While remedial measures to deal with short-term adverse social effects are required, this approach cannot be limited to the remedial. Structural adjustments are undertaken with the explicit macroeconomic objective of promoting a sustainable process of economic development. It is necessary from the outset to link the process of adjustment to the objective of promoting sustained improvement in the quality of life, in which the protection and improvement of health is an essential element. This objective has to be adopted at the very outset along with the macroeconomic objectives, and incorporated into the strategy at the stage of formulation, with a view not only to averting adverse social outcomes, but also to shaping the strategy in a way that clearly leads to a higher quality of life and a better health status at the same time as it leads to higher growth. The process of adjustment has to achieve both sets of objectives simultaneously, without any major trade-offs involving health and quality of life. Where trade-offs are unavoidable they have to be effected in the manner discussed in the preceding chapter. Remedial short-term measures themselves have to be linked to these larger long-term objectives.

What has been said about policy in the specific situation of economic adjustment applies

*Table 7: **Health expenditure before and after adjustment for 15 sub-Saharan African countries***

Country	Health expenditure as percentage of total goverment expenditure net of interest payments		Real health expenditure expressed as indices 1980 = 100	
	Before adjustment	After adjustment	Before adjustment	After adjustment
Burkino Faso	6.4	5.5	105	118
Côte d'Ivoire	3.8	4.6	97	97
Ghana	7.1	9.8	67	132
Kenya	7.6	7.1	100	99
Madagascar	5.2	5.7	61	66
Malawi	5.6	7.8	97	100
Mauritius	7.8	8.8	101	115
Niger	4.2	4.8	84	106
Nigeria	2.5	2.4	81	48
Senegal	6.0	4.9	104	113
Sierra Leone	7.2	4.0	—	—
Togo	6.4	4.8	—	—
Uganda	5.0	3.7	113	155
Zambia	7.5	5.8	100	87
Zimbabwe	6.6	6.8	135	133

1. The share of health expenditure in total government expenditure fell in 8 out of 15 countries.

2. Real health expenditure declined in 4 countries, which included 3 of the countries in category 1 above.

Source: Sahn, D. E. Fiscal and Exchange Rate Reforms in Africa – Considering the Impact on the Poor. Cornell Food and Nutrition Policy Programme, 1990.

Whether structural adjustment in Africa or economic reform in eastern Europe, vulnerable groups suffer the adverse effects.

equally to development policy in general. The principal health goals and targets have to be defined in terms of health outcome indicators, which policy-makers must constantly watch along with the macroeconomic indicators of growth, income, employment, and other components of development. This means that they must ask how development processes have helped to bring down infant and child mortality, how they have added to the average life span, how they have helped to promote demographic change and manage population growth and reproduction, how the vulnerable groups have fared under the development regime, and what has happened to malnutrition in all its forms.

When health outcomes are examined in this manner, the critical processes and key policy instruments involved do not simultaneously emerge with the identity and distinctness with which they emerge in the case of macro-economic goals. Health services, which have often been used as the crucial input and key

instrument in the case of health outcomes, are clearly inadequate for the purpose. Factors outside the control of the health services constantly intervene to constrain them in their pursuit of health goals. Their efforts are also continuously negated by new developments detrimental to health. While the definition of responsibility for health in other sectors as described earlier would help to deal with some of these problems, it still leaves many major problems unsolved. What policy-makers need is control over those elements of development policy at the macro level that can be manipulated to avoid adverse effects on health goals as well as contribute positively to the attainment of those goals.

International agencies and academic circles have recently made a considerable effort to address some of the problems by examining the impact of macroeconomic policies, particularly adjustment policies, on the lower-income groups in society. They have attempted to develop an analytical framework for studying how the effects of devaluation, cutbacks in public expenditure, monetary policies, and other structural reforms, such as those relating to the liberalization of trade, have spread down to poor households and affected their income-earning capacity, purchasing power, and health and well-being.

The studies illustrate a wide variation in outcomes, depending on the structure of the economy, the pace of reform, and the mixture of policies adopted. In some countries in which domestic agriculture has responded positively to price changes, the terms of trade have moved in favour of the rural sector and the rural poor who have benefited while the real income of the urban poor has suffered a loss, as is the case in the Gambia and Madagascar. This study, however, is focused principally on the effects on income. Efforts to identify the health impact of specific policies have been less successful, although deterioration in health and nutrition in general has been documented. Nevertheless, the work already done provides a basis for identifying the elements in macro development policies that have a direct impact on health goals and objectives.

Guidelines for the application of conditionality

How then can the concept of health conditionality be given concrete expression in policies and strategies? At the macro level, governments would need to specify targets for the improvement of health status and devise and implement development strategies to achieve them. The goals and targets would at the sectoral level become the responsibility of each sector for the avoidance of health hazards and the promotion of health in its programmes and activities. These adjustments at the macro and sectoral levels would provide guidance for the overall allocation of resources. Within such a framework the allocation of resources for health would not be subjected to the restrictive process of competing against other development sectors; the priorities for health services would emerge more forcefully and clearly than before. Responsibility for the protection and improvement of health would then be distributed more rationally within the total system in relation to potential health hazards as well as the capacity to contribute to health.

The principles that would guide resource allocation in this manner could be applied to development lending of all types. The development lending and assistance of the international community would have to encourage the process by including improvement of health status as one element of conditionality and take adequate account of it in resource allocations made to support adjustments. All major development programmes could include an element of conditionality for health related to the health impact of the programmes. Resource allocations could be included in projects for the specific purpose of enhancing their capacity to contribute to health. The lending for sector adjustment by the World Bank provides scope for supporting the effort needed at the national level to restructure existing systems so that countries can focus effectively on the improvement of health status as an integral part of development.

Mitigating social costs of structural adjustment

In the late 1980s several governments designed and implemented special programmes to ease the introduction of difficult adjustment measures and compensate for their adverse impact on disadvantaged groups. Among them two of the better-known examples of well-developed, multisectoral efforts are those of Bolivia and Ghana. Bolivia's Emergency Social Fund (ESF) operates through a special agency designed for the purpose — a domestic financing institution for projects selected by local communities and implemented by private contractors. Ghana's programme of action to mitigate the social costs of adjustment works with well-established government agencies. It includes more than 20 anti-poverty measures covering public works to provide employment, credit, training, low-cost water supply, drugs for health care, nutrition, and shelter, all with a strong orientation towards community involvement and the participation of indigenous NGOs. It has three major objectives — enhancing the purchasing power of the poor, imparting basic skills, and protecting health. Though the programme focuses on the short-term social effects of stabilization and structural adjustment, it has links with the longer-term strategies and interventions needed for the transformation of the vulnerable groups.

Since then a number of countries such as Cameroon, the Gambia, Guinea, and Madagascar have designed compensatory programmes for public sector employees laid off as a result of budget cuts and social action initiatives in the field of health, food, nutrition, education, and women in development. The Gambia has set up an operation for promoting small-scale and medium-scale enterprises which has a special component focusing on enterprises for women. Guinea is establishing an informal sector micro-credit mechanism through NGOs. Cameroon is developing a social action programme that includes projects for population, health, education, employment, women in development, and community development. Based on earlier prototypes (especially the Bolivian ESF), social action funds have been or are being established as part of adjustment programmes in several countries including Guinea, Malawi, and Mozambique.

Source: World Bank, *World Development Report 1990*, and section on Social Action Programmes, pages 178-179 of *Structural Adjustment and Poverty, A Conceptual, Empirical and Policy Framework* 1990. Report no. 8393–AFR (restricted circulation World Bank document not available to the public), Washington, D.C., 1990

Chapter 7
Conclusions

Health is an essential part of the quality of life, which is the overall goal of development. It is at the base of all economic activities and processes of development and is integral to the state of well-being human beings must possess to realize their full human potential and derive satisfaction from their normal life situation. The protection and improvement of health must therefore be a central objective in all development strategies. Health is part of development in the same way as the environment is part of development. It has to be integrated into development policy with the same constant concern and attention as has been shown in relation to the environment.

Although there is a growing awareness of the importance of health in development, a wide gap still exists between this awareness and its concrete expression in development strategies and policies. This is partly due to the tendency to rely on the health services to deal with the health effects of economic development and the failure to take account of health needs and effects at the stage at which development policies are formulated. The result is on the one hand a steady influx of new health hazards and on the other escalating health care costs. The model of health care that has evolved with the increasing sophistication of health technology is proving to be unsustainable even for developed countries; it imposes unmanageable burdens for the developing countries. To remedy the situation, the formulation and implementation of development policies at all levels – global, national, local – must continuously take account of the health effects, adjusting the health goals to the other important development goals and achieving them simultaneously with the others.

An essential condition in this approach to health and development is that a country or community should identify its profile of vulnerability and the changes taking place in that profile. Within the profile it must then identify the highly vulnerable groups.

In almost all situations of acute or high vulnerability, four basic conditions recur in varying combinations but form a single closely interlinked matrix of vulnerability in which each condition reinforces and perpetuates the other. It is possible to observe this matrix in national situations, as in countries with low human development indicators. But, in order to understand the interrelationships in their full complexity, it is necessary to identify them as they exist at the micro level in local communities and in the vulnerable groups within them. These four conditions are: poor health status; lack of functional literacy, in the wider sense of the knowledge and skill to move out of the condition of vulnerability; low productivity and income-earning capacity; and a general helplessness and incapacity to gain access to and control over resources. The micro-level strategies aimed at transforming the vulnerable groups have to aim simultaneously at improving their condition through the improvement of health status, functional literacy, and access to economic resources. To achieve this, new approaches are required to integrate these strategies in development policies and strategies at all levels, micro, macro, and global.

The profiles of vulnerability in countries vary with their socioeconomic conditions and health situation as do the nature and distribution of the vulnerable groups themselves. What is important, however, is that the condition of vulnerability and highly vulnerable groups exist in varying forms in all countries, both developed and developing, though the most severe manifestations of vulnerabililty occur in developing countries.

Highly vulnerable groups are a crucial element in all development strategies. The propensity to vulnerability and the structures of deprivation that exist in a society find their most acute manifestation in such groups. By analysing the conditions of their vulnerability and working out strategies for their transformation, some of the major constraints to social, economic, and political development can be removed. The vulnerable groups are themselves human resources that have been neglected and marginalized in most economic development strategies. In developing countries in particular they form a large proportion of the population. Enabling them to realize their full human potential would make a significant difference to economic growth and the process of development as a whole.

In this approach, health status assumes a place of equal value and importance to that of other elements. In most integrated strategies, health is approached as an element to be added in the form of improvement and expansion of the

health services, or as a plus value to the outcome, not as an integral part of the process of transformation. Health status provides the best mode of entry into assessment of the total condition of vulnerability in any given society and community, revealing the other conditions of deprivation and helping to identify development needs. It also provides an exit point, in the sense that improvement of health status is the best indicator that the development processes are succeeding in transforming the vulnerable groups and lifting them out of their vulnerable condition. The changes in health status of the vulnerable groups then become an indispensable criterion both in the formulation of national development policies and strategies and in evaluation of their outcomes. The mixture of health status indicators that has to be selected for identifying vulnerable groups and monitoring the changes will vary with the profile of vulnerability appropriate to the country. In most developing countries, health status indicators relating to women in the childbearing phase of life will probably be the most important component and this group and their vulnerability state will assume strategic significance. Monitoring the health status of the highly vulnerable groups will have to form part of the regular surveillance of health. Development policies will have to respond by continuous adjustment to what is revealed in the process of monitoring.

Integration of health goals and improvement of health status in development strategy and policy depend crucially on capacity to effect trade-offs between health and economic development. Trade-offs will be inevitable. In some cases health costs may have to be incurred in the short term to secure substantial economic gains that bring major long-term health benefits. In others it may be necessary to forego some part of potential economic gains to avoid serious long-term impairment to health. What is necessary is a system of choice and decision-making ensuring that choice is constantly disciplined by efforts to achieve the health and economic goals simultaneously. If trade-offs become inevitable, they should be short-term and made good as quickly as possible so as to restore the conditions for good health. Adequate information has to be provided for the choices. This process of decision-making implies that a national account of the trade-offs is maintained and closely monitored. There is a growing body of knowledge on the health costs of economic development programmes and policies and it will enable governments to begin working towards these objectives.

An important means of ensuring that economic choices and development decisions are linked to health objectives lies in resource allocation itself, health becoming a part of the basic conditions stipulated for the allocation of resources for development. Health then becomes part of the conditionality governing development. Several initiatives and approaches are possible. At the macro level, every major allocation for development could have specific health objectives, which would be made a condition of the allocation and ensure that health objectives were integrated within the sectoral policies. These allocations could also include resources earmarked for specific health-promoting and health-protecting activities, which can best be undertaken as an integral part of the sectoral activities and which are normally neglected or given low priority when left to intrasectoral resource allocation. Governments and international lending agencies could adopt similar approaches. Financial institutions could incorporate health objectives into their lending by including an appropriate health component in the conditions attached to loans, incorporating a

health activity as part of the package of investments financed by the loan, and avoiding investments that could have harmful effects on health. The main problem is to link the major financial outlays made for an increase of income and improved economic well-being at the micro or macro level to the need for the protection and promotion of health so that concern for health and recognition of its value become an integral part of economic decision-making.

The issues that have been discussed have a global dimension, whether they concern changing patterns of vulnerability or the model of health care that has been evolving in response to them. The issues are similar in character to those related to the environment, which have claimed attention at the global level. Health issues have often been linked to environmental issues and have been subsumed under concern about the sustainability of development. But health issues need to be recognized in their own right. There is a growing awareness that development, as it has taken place, does not provide a solution to the unsatisfactory state of health that preceded it. The widespread impairment of human health by environmental degradation, the grave health risks of technological advances such as nuclear technology and biotechnology, the AIDS pandemic, the rapidity with which outbreaks of disease assume epidemic proportions in entire regions (such as the recent cholera epidemic in Latin America), and the unpredictable consequences of changing lifestyles are among the numerous developments that have helped to promote this awareness. It is this awareness that needs to find expression in the integration of health in development strategies at the global and national levels, in the same way as environmental strategies have been integrated. Global surveillance of human health has to be similar to that of the environment and concerned not only with the effects of development but also with crucial health-endangering processes.

A final question may have profound relevance to the place health issues must assume in the future adjustments that need to be made. It has been compellingly demonstrated that there is no easy way to reconcile the goals and expectations of economic development with the inescapable needs of the environment. It is evident that the carrying capacity of the planet cannot sustain development and the corresponding lifestyle of the wealthy industrialized countries if these are replicated on a global scale. On the other hand, a sustainable model of development requires a set of disciplines that must eventually be universally applicable and capable of promoting a lifestyle that in its essential elements is replicable on a global scale. The adjustments needed will require a shift of concern from quantitative expansion of goods and services to quality of life. This will call for far-reaching changes both in the expectations and goals of development in developing countries and in the prevailing lifestyles of the developed countries. Can global concern about human health help in evolving the model needed to promote such processes of adjustment?

Selected bibliography

Alderman, H. *Nutritional status in Ghana and its determinants*. Cornell Food and Nutrition Policy Programme Working Paper No. 1. New York, Cornell Food and Nutrition Policy Programme, 1990.

Central Bank of Sri Lanka. *Annual Report 1990*. Colombo, Central Bank Press, 1991.

Children's Defense Fund. *The State of America's Children 1991*. Washington, D.C., 1991.

Cooper Weil, D. et al. *The Impact of Development Policies on Health: A Review of the Literature*. Geneva, World Health Organization, 1990.

Demery, L., Addison, T. *The Alleviation of Poverty Under Structural Adjustment*. Washington, D.C., World Bank, 1987.

Department of Census & Statistics, Sri Lanka. *Demographic & Health Survey 1987*. Colombo, 1987.

Dorosh, P. et al. *Macroeconomic Adjustment and the Poor: The Case of Madagascar*. Cornell Food and Nutrition Policy Programme Monograph No. 9. New York, Cornell Food and Nutrition Policy Programme, 1990.

Gunatilleke, G. (ed.). *Intersectoral Linkages and Health Development: Case Studies in India (Kerala State), Jamaica, Norway, Sri Lanka and Thailand*. Offset Publication No. 83. Geneva, World Health Organization, 1984.

Holt, S.L., Ribe, H. *Developing Financial Institutions for the Poor and Reducing Barriers to Access for Women*. World Bank Discussion Paper No. 117. Washington, D.C., World Bank, 1991.

Jabara, C.L. *Economic Reform and Poverty in the Gambia: A Survey of Pre and Post ERP Experience*. New York, Cornell Food and Nutrition Policy Programme, 1990.

Labonte, R., "Econology: Integrating Health and Sustainable Development – Part One: Theory & Background". *Health Promotion International*, 1991, 6: 49-65.

Matte, T.D. et al. "Lead Poisoning Among Household Members Exposed to Lead-acid Battery Repair Shops in Kingston, Jamaica". *International Journal of Epidemiology*, 1989, 18: 874-81.

Ministry of Health, Sri Lanka – *Annual Health Bulletin, 1990*. Colombo, 1990.

National Commission on Children. *Beyond Rhetoric. A New American Agenda for Children and Families*. Washington, D.C., 1991.

Pinstrup-Andersen, P. *Food Subsidies in Developing Countries: Costs, Benefits and Policy Options*. Baltimore, Johns Hopkins University Press, 1988.

Rahman, A. *Impact of Grameen Bank on the Nutritional Status of the Rural Poor*. Research report no. 108. Bangladesh Institute of Development Studies, 1989 (unpublished document).

German Commission for Justice and Peace and the Grameen Bank. *International Dialogue and Exposure Programme*. Bangladesh, 14-22 October, 1989.

Rajeandran & Reich, M.R. "Environmental Health in Malaysia". *Bulletin of the Atomic Scientists,* 1981, 37(4): 30-35.

Sahn, D.E. *Fiscal and Exchange Rate Reform in Africa – Considering the Impact Upon the Poor*. New York, Cornell Food and Nutrition Policy Programme, 1990.

UNICEF. *State of the World's Children 1991*. New York, Oxford University Press, 1991.

United Nations Development Programme. *Human Development Report 1990*. New York, Oxford University Press. 1990.

United Nations Development Programme. *Human Development Report 1991*. New York, Oxford University Press. 1991.

United Nations Office at Vienna, Centre for Social Development & Humanitarian Affairs. *The World Aging Situation 1991*. Vienna, 1992.

World Bank. *Structural Adjustment and Poverty: A Conceptual, Empirical and Policy Framework*. Report No. 8393-AFR (restricted circulation World Bank document not available to the public). Washington, D.C., 1990.

World Bank. *World Development Report 1982*. New York, Oxford University Press, 1982.

World Bank. *World Development Report 1990*. New York, Oxford University Press, 1990.

World Bank. *World Development Report 1991*. New York, Oxford University Press, 1991.

World Health Organization. *The Implications of Public Policy on Health Status and Quality of Life*. Report of a symposium held in Bangalore, India, 18-26 October, 1989. New Delhi, 1989.

World Health Organization. *Intersectoral Action for Health: The Role of Intersectoral Cooperation in National Strategies for Health for All*. Geneva, 1986.

World Health Organization. *World Health Statistics Annual 1990*. Geneva, 1991.

World Health Organization. *Women, Health and Development*. Progress report by the Director-General for the 44th World Health Assembly. Geneva, 1991.

World Health Organization. *Current and Future Dimensions of the HIV/AIDS Pandemic – A Capsule Summary*. Geneva, 1991.

World Health Organization. *Basic Documents, 38th Edition*. Geneva, 1990.

Newspaper article credits *(articles reprinted by permission)*

Page 4   *La Tribune de Genève*. "Le tiers monde viellit à son tour". Laszlo Molnar. 25 July 1991.

Page 7   *La Tribune de Genève*. "L'alcool aggrave le sous-développement". 9 July 1991.

Page 8   *Associated Press (International News)*. "Economic Austerity Throws Latin America into Recession". Barry Lynn. 17 October 1990.

Page 10   *The Boston Globe*. "At forum, Flynn urges that violence be seen as a public health issue". Alexander Reid. April 27 1991.

Page 10   *Sunday Nation*. "Why strikes and Kizito tragedy had to happen". Wamahiu Muya. 21 July 1991.

Page 15   *La Suisse*. "Progression du sida vers le sud". 18 June 1991.

Page 15   *La Tribune de Genève*. "Sida/1000 chercheurs réunis à Florence – Assis sur un volcan". 17 June 1991.

Page 16   *Post Courier*. "Dreaded malaria on the increase around the world". 14 June 1991.

Page 23   *International Herald Tribune*. "America's Weigh In: Still Lots of Fat to Lose". William Booth. 15 July 1991.

Page 23   *The Guardian*. "Traffic fumes 'asthma risk for children'". Daniel John. 29 July 1991.

Page 23   *International Herald Tribune*. "Juvenile Diabetes Puzzling Peaks". Robin Herman. 18 July 1991.

Page 25   *St Louis Daily Record*. "National experts urge link for health and education". Janet Bass. 31 May 1991.

Page 25   *Education Week*. "Education and Health Sectors Are Urged to Cooperate To Ensure Child's Success". Ellen Flax.

Page 26   *World Watch*. "Sanitation in the Time of Cholera". Ann Misch. July/August 1991.

Page 29   *Arlac Newsletter*. "Illiteracy can be deadly". June 1991.

Page 29   *Washington Times*. "Study says half of high school grads lack skill to work well". Laura M. Litvan. 3 July 1991.

Page 41   *Wall Street Journal*. "Microloans to Entrepeneurs are growing in Third World". Brent Bowers. (The article appeared in the Wall Street Journal Europe, issue 13 June 1991. Reprinted by permission of the Wall Street Journal Europe. © 1991 Dow Jones and Company Inc. All rights reserved worldwide).

Page 41   *African Business*. "Refugee enterprises pay dividends in Sudan. March 1990.

Page 44   *Le Monde Diplomatique*. "Drogue, banlieues, intégrismes". René Passet. August 1991.

Page 51   *Los Angeles Times*. "Workfare Found to Save Money, Not Ease Poverty". Virginia Ellis. 24 July 1991. Copyright 1991, Los Angeles Times.

Page 52   *China Daily*. "Cigarette firms aim at Third World sales". 18 June 1991.

Page 54   *Journal de Genève*. "Mexico: le cancer de la pollution et du centralisme". Jean-Pierre Bastian. 17 June 1991.

Page 55   *International Herald Tribune*. "Naming Eco-Managers German Firms Go Green" Ferdinand Protzman. 11 July 1991.

Page 59   *Masvingo Provincial Star*. "PSA Voices fears about Structural Adjustment". 7 June 1991.

Page 59   *Le Monde*. "Une génération d'enfants en péril". Isabelle Vichniac. 10 July 1991.

SOCIAL SCIENCE LIBRARY

Manor Road Building
Manor Road
Oxford OX1 3UQ
Tel: (2)71093 (enquiries and renewals)
http://www.ssl.ox.ac.uk

This is a NORMAL LOAN item.

We will email you a reminder before this item is due.

Please see http://www.ssl.ox.ac.uk/lending.html
for details on:

- loan policies; these are also displayed on the notice boards and in our library guide.

- how to check when your books are due back.

- how to renew your books, including information on the maximum number of renewals. Items may be renewed if not reserved by another reader. Items must be renewed before the library closes on the due date.

- level of fines; fines are charged on overdue books.

Please note that this item may be recalled during Term.

WITHDRAWN

← BARCODE